Contents

Getting started

On the 30th of September 2005, a series of cartoons appeared in a Danish newspaper.

The cartoons showed images of the prophet Muhammad and hinted at a connection with Islamic terrorism. However, it was not before the end of January 2006 that, with the help of the Internet, the reaction spread worldwide and became militant. What had started as a controversy over the freedom of the press and respect of religious beliefs turned into a "clash of civilisations".

1. Sum up in a few sentences what you remember about the controversy which started with the cartoons.
2. Briefly sketch your own attitude.
3. Comment on these two pages, particularly on the cartoon on the right.

Ethnicity and identity

Bernard Malamud, The Lady of the Lake

Bernard Malamud's short story is, on the face of things, about love gone wrong. A young man from New York decides to travel to Europe, hoping to find a girl to marry there. In Italy he finds Isabella and falls in love with her. She obviously feels the same way. So what has gone wrong? At a very early stage in their relationship, Isabella asks him if he is a Jew. He denies this although, as the reader knows, he is one. While the love relation slowly develops and the idea of marriage is not only on Henry's mind but also seems to be attractive for Isabella, his denial begins to worry Henry more and more. Nevertheless, he does not fully comprehend the significance of his lie for his future happiness – until the final encounter.

The first-person narrator's change of name, from the typical Jewish name of Levin to the telling name of Freeman, almost inconspicuously prepares the reader for the significance of personal identity and the acceptance of one's historical and cultural past in this story. In the course of the story, the question of Henry's cultural and religious identity is frequently raised and makes one think of the biblical example of the question put to Saint Peter – and of his failure (cf. the reference to the leper in Dante's *Inferno*). Isabella in her reaction to this essential question not only points out another possible attitude to the past but also gives the only answer that has made survival possible for the Jews in the diaspora: – to preserve the past, which makes suffering meaningful.

diaspora movement of Jewish people away from their own country to live in other countries

to walk the floor here: to work in a (book) shop

lapel [lə'pel] Revers

inheritance what your ancestors leave behind
to inherit, heritage; heir

The motif of name-giving. ➔ What does it reveal about Levin?

Henry Levin, an ambitious, handsome thirty, who walked the floors in Macy's book department wearing a white flower in his lapel, having recently come into a small inheritance, quit, and went abroad seeking romance. In Paris, for no reason he was sure of, except that he was tired of the past – tired of the limitations it had imposed upon him; although he had signed the hotel register with his right name, Levin took to calling himself Henry R. Freeman. Freeman lived for a short while in a little hotel on a narrow gas lamp-lit street near the Luxembourg Gardens. In the beginning he liked the sense of foreignness of the city – of things different, anything likely to happen. He liked, he said to himself, the possible combinations. But not much did happen; he met no one he particularly cared for (he had sometimes in the past deceived himself about women, they had come to less than he had expected); and since the heat was hot and tourists underfoot, he felt he must flee. He boarded the Milan express, and after Dijon, developed a painful, palpitating anxiety. This grew so troublesome that he had serious visions of leaping off the train, but reason prevailed and he rode on. However, he did not get to Milan. Nearing Stresa, after a quick, astonished look at Lake Maggiore, Freeman, a nature lover from early childhood, pulled his suitcase off the rack and hurriedly left the train. He at once felt better.

An hour later he was established in a pensione in a villa not far from the line of assorted hotels fronting the Stresa shore. The padrona, a talkative woman, much interested in her guests, complained that June and July had been lost in unseasonable cold and wet. Many had cancelled; there were few Americans around. This didn't exactly disturb Freeman, who had had his full share of Coney Island. He lived in an airy, French-windowed room, including soft bed and spacious bath, and though personally the shower type, was glad of the change. He was very fond of the balcony at his window, where he loved to read, or study Italian, glancing up often to gaze at the water. The long blue lake, sometimes green, sometimes gold, went out of sight among distant mountains. He liked the red-roofed town of Pallanza on the opposite shore, and especially the four beautiful islands in the water, tiny but teeming with palazzi, tall trees, gardens, visible statuary. The sight of these islands aroused in Freeman a deep emotion; each a universe – how often do we come across one in a lifetime? – filled him with expectancy. Of what, he wasn't sure. Freeman still hoped for what he hadn't, what few got in the world and many dared not think of; to wit, love, adventure, freedom. Alas, the words by now sounded slightly comical. Yet there were times, when he was staring at the islands, if you pushed him a little he could almost cry. Ah, what names of beauty: Isola Bella, dei Pescatori, Madre, and del Dongo. Travel is truly broadening, he thought; who ever got emotional over Welfare Island?

But the islands, the two he visited, let him down. Freeman walked off the vaporetto at Isola Bella amid a crowd of late-season tourists in all languages, especially German, who were at once beset by many vendors of cheap trinkets. And he

underfoot here: in the way

➔ Look for the deeper meaning of *flee.*

palpitating here: strongly felt

to prevail to be stronger in influence

Coney Island resort section of New York City, formerly an island

French-windowed *mit bis zum Boden reichenden Flügelfenstern*

statuary collection of statues

vaporetto (It.) *Boot*

beset attacked from all sides

trinket object of little value

junk here: *Kitsch*
crooked winding
dory boat with a flat bottom

discovered there were guided tours only – strictly no unsupervised wandering – the pink palazzo full of old junk, surrounded by artificial formal gardens, including grottoes made of seashells, the stone statuary a tasteless laugh. And although Isola dei Pescatori had some honest atmosphere, old houses hugging crooked streets, thick nets drying in piles near fishermen's dories drawn up among trees; again there were tourists snapping all in pictures, and the whole town catering to them. Everybody had something to sell you could buy better in Macy's basement. Freeman returned to his pensione, disappointed. The islands, beautiful from afar, up close were so much stage scenery. He complained thus to the padrona and she urged him to visit Isola del Dongo. "More natural," she persuaded him. "You never saw such unusual gardens. And the palazzo is historical, full of the tombs of famous men of the region, including a cardinal who became a saint. Napoleon, the emperor, slept there. The French have always loved this island. Their writers have wept at its beauty."

laden very full

However, Freeman showed little interest. "Gardens I've seen in my time." So, when restive, he wandered in the back streets of Stresa, watching the men playing at boccia, avoiding the laden store windows. Drifting by devious routes back to the lake, he sat at a bench in the small park, watching the lingering sunset over the dark mountains and thinking of a life of adventure. He watched alone, talked now and then to stray Italians – almost everybody spoke a good broken English – and lived too much on himself. On weekends, there was, however, a buzz of merriment in the streets. Excursionists from around Milan arrived in busloads. All day they hurried to their picnics; at night one of them pulled an accordion out of the bus and played sad Venetian or happy Neapolitan songs. Then the young Italians and their girls got up and danced in tight embrace in the public square; but not Freeman.

for want of not having
dread oppressive fear

One evening at sunset, the calm waters so marvelously painted they drew him from inactivity, he hired a rowboat, and for want of anyplace more exciting to go, rowed toward the Isola del Dongo. He had no intention other than reaching it, then turning back, a round trip completed. Two-thirds of the way there, he began to row with growing uneasiness which soon became dread, because a stiff breeze had risen, driving the sucking waves against the side of the boat. It was a warm wind, but a wind was a wind and the water was wet. Freeman didn't row well – had learned late in his twenties, despite the nearness of Central Park – and he swam poorly, always swallowing water, never enough breath to get anywhere; clearly a landlubber from the word go. He strongly considered returning to Stresa – it was at least a half mile to the island, then a mile and a half in return – but chided himself for his timidity. He had, after all, hired the boat for an hour; so he kept rowing though he feared the risk. However, the waves were not too bad and he had discovered the trick of letting them hit the prow head-on. Although he handled his oars awkwardly, Freeman, to his surprise, made good time. The wind now helped rather than hindered; and daylight – reassuring – still lingered in the sky among streaks of red.

At last Freeman neared the island. Like Isola Bella, it rose in terraces through hedged gardens crowded with statuary, to a palazzo on top. But the padrona had told the truth – this island looked more interesting than the others, the vegetation lush, wilder, exotic birds flying around. By now the place was bathed in mist, and despite the thickening dark, Freeman recaptured the sense of awe and beauty he had felt upon first beholding the islands. At the same time he recalled a sad memory of unlived life, his own, of all that had slipped through his fingers. Amidst these thoughts he was startled by a movement in the garden by the water's edge. It had momentarily seemed as though a statue had come to life, but Freeman quickly realized a woman was standing this side of a low marble wall, watching the water. He could not, of course, make out her face, though he sensed she was young; only the skirt of her white dress moved in the breeze. He imagined someone waiting for her lover, and was tempted to speak to her, but then the wind blew up strongly and the waves rocked his rowboat. Freeman hastily turned the boat with one oar, and pulling hard, took off. The wind drenched him with spray, the rowboat bobbed among nasty waves, the going grew frighteningly rough. He had visions of drowning, the rowboat swamped, poor Freeman slowly sinking to the bottom, striving fruitlessly to reach the top. But as he rowed, his heart like a metal disk in his mouth, and still rowed on, gradually he overcame his fears; also the waves and wind. Although the lake was by now black, though the sky still dimly reflected white, turning from time to time to peer ahead, he guided himself by the flickering lights of the Stresa shore. It rained hard as he landed, but Freeman, as he beached the boat, considered his adventure an accomplishment and ate a hearty supper at an expensive restaurant.

The curtains billowing in his sunny room the next morning, awoke him. Freeman rose, shaved, bathed, and after breakfast got a haircut. Wearing his bathing trunks under slacks, he

landlubber sb clumsy at sea
from the word go from the very beginning
to chide to show disapproval
timidity fear

prow the bow of a ship
oar wooden pole with which you row

How is the reader prepared for the special encounter to follow?

to behold (fml) to see

to be tempted to feel like doing sth you shouldn't do
tempter, temptress; temptable, temptation

to drench to make very wet

to billow to move in waves

dip brief plunge into the water

to snatch a snooze have a quick nap

lanky tall and thin with long limbs

raft *Floß*

gewgaw valueless article

vietato (It.) forbidden

jaunty stylish

cane (walking) stick

clip speed

elaborate refined
to elaborate, elaboration

counterpane *Trennscheibe*

wrathful full of anger

parasol small umbrella protecting against sunrays

voluptuous splendid, rich

profusion extravagant display

intoxicating almost drowning the senses
toxic (poisonous) **intoxication**

fragrance nice smell

off one's rocker in a state of extreme confusion

assailment overpowering attack

sneaked onto the Hotel Excelsior beach for a dip, short but refreshing. In the early afternoon he read his Italian lesson on the balcony, then snatched a snooze. At four-thirty – he felt he really hadn't made up his mind until then – Freeman boarded the vaporetto making its hourly tour of the islands. After touching at Isola Madre, the boat headed for the Isola del Dongo. As they were approaching the island, coming from the direction opposite that which Freeman had taken last night, he observed a lanky boy in bathing trunks sunning himself on a raft in the lake – nobody he recognized. When the vaporetto landed at the dock on the southern side of the island, to Freeman's surprise and deep regret, the area was crowded with the usual stalls piled high with tourist gewgaws. And though he had hoped otherwise, inspection of the island was strictly in the guide's footsteps, and *vietato* trying to go anywhere alone. You paid a hundred lire for a ticket, then trailed behind this unshaven, sad-looking clown, who stabbed a jaunty cane at the sky as he announced in three languages to the tourists who followed him: "Please not stray nor wander. The family del Dongo, one of the most illustrious of Italy, so requests. Only thus ees eet able to remain open thees magnificent 'eestorical palatz and supreme jardens for the inspection by the members of all nations."

They tailed the guide at a fast clip through the palace, through long halls hung with tapestries and elaborate mirrors, enormous rooms filled with antique furniture, old books, paintings, statuary – a lot of it in better taste than the stuff he had seen on the other island; and he visited where Napoleon had slept – a bed. Yet Freeman secretly touched the counterpane, though not quickly enough to escape the all-seeing eye of the Italian guide, who wrathfully raised his cane to the level of Freeman's heart and explosively shouted, " Basta!" This embarrassed Freeman and two British ladies carrying parasols. He felt bad until the group – about twenty – were led into the garden. Gazing from here, the highest point of the island, at the panorama of the golden-blue lake, Freeman gasped. And the luxuriant vegetation of the island was daring, voluptuous. They went among orange and lemon trees (he had never known that lemon was a perfume), magnolia, oleander – the guide called out the names. Everywhere were flowers in great profusion, huge camellias, rhododendron, jasmine, roses in innumerable colors and varieties, all bathed in intoxicating floral fragrance. Freeman's head swam; he felt dizzy, slightly off his rocker at this extraordinary assailment of his senses. At the same time, though it was an "underground" reaction, he experienced a painful, contracting remembrance – more like a warning – of personal poverty. This he had difficulty accounting for, because he usually held a decent opinion of himself. When the comical guide bounced forward, with his cane indicating cedars, eucalyptus, camphor and pepper trees, the former floorwalker, overcome by all he was for the first time seeing, at the same moment choked by almost breathless excitement, fell behind the group of tourists, and pretended to inspect the berries of a pepper tree. As the guide hurried forward, Freeman, although not positive he had planned it so, ducked behind the pepper tree, ran along a path beside a tall laurel shrub and down two flights of stairs; he hopped over a marble wall and went hastily through a small wood, expectant, seeking, he thought only God knew what.

He figured he was headed in the direction of the garden by the water where he had seen the girl in the white dress last night, but after several minutes of involved wandering, Freeman came upon a little beach, a pebbly strand, leading down stone steps into the lake. About a hundred feet away a raft was anchored, nobody on it. Exhausted by the excitement, a little moody, Freeman sat down under a tree, to rest. When he glanced up, a girl in a white bathing suit was coming up the steps out of the water. Freeman stared as she sloshed up the shore, her wet skin glistening in bright sunlight. She had seen him and quickly bent for a towel she had left on a blanket, draped it over her shoulders and modestly held the ends together over her high-arched breast. Her wet black hair fell upon her shoulders. She stared at Freeman. He rose, forming words of apology in his mind. A haze that had been before his eyes, evaporated. Freeman grew pale and the girl blushed.

Freeman was, of course, a New York City boy from away back. As the girl stood there unselfconsciously regarding him – it could not have been longer than thirty seconds – he was aware of his background and certain other disadvantages; but he also knew he wasn't a bad-looking guy, even, it could be said, quite on the handsome side. Though a pinprick bald at the back of his noggin – not more than a dime could adequately cover – his head of hair was alive, expressive; Freeman's gray eyes were clear, unenvious, nose well-molded, the mouth generous. He had well-proportioned arms and legs and his stomach lay respectfully flat. He was a bit short, but on him, he knew, it barely showed. One of his former girl friends had told him she sometimes thought of him as tall. This counterbalanced the occasions when he had thought of him-

to choke to take one's breath away

laurel *Lorbeer*
shrub bush

moody slightly sad

to slosh up to splash through water

apology excuse
to apologise, apologetic

haze slight mist

Analyse the description of both Freeman's and the girl's situation and state of mind.

pinprick small mark
bald having no hair
noggin (AE) here: head

self as short. Yet though he knew he made a good appearance, Freeman feared this moment, partly because of all he hungered for from life, and partly because of the uncountable obstacles existing between strangers, may the word forever perish.

She, apparently, had no fear of their meeting; as a matter of surprising fact, seemed to welcome it, immediately curious about him. She had, of course, the advantage of position – which included receiving, so to speak, the guest-intruder. And she had grace to lean on; herself also favored physically – mama, what a queenly high-assed form – itself the cause of grace. Her dark, sharp Italian face had that quality of beauty which holds the mark of history, the beauty of a people and civilization. The large brown eyes, under straight slender brows, were filled with sweet light; her lips were purely cut as if from red flowers; her nose was perhaps the one touch of imperfection that perfected the rest – a trifle long and thin. Despite the effect, a little of sculpture, her ovoid face, tapering to a small chin, was soft, suffused with the loveliness of youth. She was about twenty-three or -four. And when Freeman had, to a small degree, calmed down, he discovered in her eyes a hidden hunger, or memory thereof; perhaps it was sadness; and he felt he was, for this reason, if not unknown others, sincerely welcomed. Had he, Oh God, at last met his fate?

ovoid oval-shaped

suffused here: full of

"Si è perduto?" the girl asked, smiling, still tightly holding her white towel. Freeman understood and answered in English. "No, I came on my own. On purpose you might say." He had in mind to ask her if she remembered having seen him before, namely in last night's rowboat, but didn't.

si è perduto (It.) are you lost

"Are you an American?" she inquired, her Italian accent pleasantly touched with an English one.

"That's right."

The girl studied him for a full minute, and then hesitantly asked, "Are you, perhaps, Jewish?"

The girl's fateful question ➜ and his reaction.

Freeman suppressed a groan. Though secretly shocked by the question, it was not, in a way, unexpected. Yet he did not look Jewish, could pass as not – had. So without batting an eyelash, he said, no, he wasn't. And a moment later added, though he personally had nothing against them.

"It was just a thought. You Americans are so varied," she explained vaguely.

"I understand," he said, "but have no worry." Lifting his hat, he introduced himself: "Henry R. Freeman, travelling abroad."

"My name," she said, after an absent-minded pause, "is Isabella del Dongo."

Safe on first, thought Freeman. "I'm proud to know you." He bowed. She gave him her hand with a gentle smile. He was about to surprise it with a kiss when the comical guide appeared at a wall a few terraces above. He gazed at them in astonishment, then let out a yell and ran down the stairs, waving his cane like a rapier.

rapier *Klinge*

"Transgressor," he shouted at Freeman.

transgressor sb acting against the law
to transgress, transgression

The girl said something to calm him, but the guide was too furious to listen. He grabbed Freeman's arm, yanking him toward the stairs. And though Freeman, in the interest of good manners, barely resisted, the guide whacked him across the seat of the pants; but the ex-floorwalker did not complain.

to yank to pull quickly

ex-floorwalker a former (book) shop assistant

Though his departure from the island had been, to put it mildly, an embarrassment (the girl had vanished after her unsuccessful momentary intercession), Freeman dreamed of a triumphant return. The big thing so far was that she, a knockout, had taken to him; he had been favored by her. Just why, he couldn't exactly tell, but he could tell yes, had seen in her eyes. Yet wondering if yes why yes – an old habit – Freeman, among other reasons he had already thought of, namely the thus and therefore of man-woman attraction – laid it to the fact that he was different, had dared. He had, specifically, dared to duck the guide and be waiting for her at the edge of the lake when she came out of it. And she was different too, (which of course quickened her response to him). Not only in her looks and background, but of course different as regards past. (He had been reading with fascination about the del Dongos in all the local guide books.) Her past he could see boiling in her all the way back to the knights of old, and then some; his own history was something else again, but men were malleable, and he wasn't afraid of attempting to create certain daring combinations: Isabella and Henry Freeman. Hoping to meet someone like her was his main reason for having come abroad. And he had also felt he would be appreciated more by a European woman; his personality, that is. Yet, since their lives were *so* different, Freeman had moments of grave doubt, wondered what trials he was in for if he went after her, as he had every intention of doing: with her unknown family – other things of that sort. And he was in afterthought worried because she had asked him if he was Jewish. Why had the question popped out of her pretty mouth before they had even met? He had never before been asked anything like this by a girl, under let's call it similar circumstances. Just when they were looking each other over. He was

knockout (ifml) very attractive

malleable can be shaped, influenced

His reasons for coming – and his doubts.

puzzled because he absolutely did not look Jewish. But then he figured her question might have been a "test" of some kind, she making it a point, when a man attracted her, quickly to determine his "eligibility." Maybe she had once had some sort of unhappy experience with a Jew? Unlikely, but possible, they were now everywhere. Freeman finally explained it to himself as "one of those things," perhaps a queer thought that had for no good reason impulsively entered her mind. And because it was queer, his answer, without elaboration, was sufficient. With ancient history why bother? All these things – the odds against him, whetted his adventurous appetite.

eligibility suitability as a partner

to whet to stimulate

He was in the grip of an almost unbearable excitement and must see her again soon, often, become her friend – not more than a beginning but where begin? He considered calling her on the telephone, if there was one in a palazzo where Napoleon had slept. But if the maid or somebody answered the phone first, he would have a ridiculous time identifying himself; so he settled for sending her a note. Freeman wrote a few lines on good stationery he had bought for the purpose, asking if he might have the pleasure of seeing her again under circumstances favorable to leisurely conversation. He suggested a carriage ride to one of the other lakes in the neighborhood, and signed his name not Levin, of course, but Freeman. Later he told the padrona that anything addressed to that name was meant for him. She was always to refer to him as Mr. Freeman. He gave no explanation, although the padrona raised interested brows; but after he had slipped her – for reasons of friendship – a thousand lire, her expression became serene. Having mailed the letter, he felt time descend on him like an intricate trap. How would he ever endure until she answered? That evening he impatiently hired a rowboat and headed for Isola del Dongo. The water was glassy smooth but when he arrived, the palazzo was dark, almost gloomy, not a single window lit; the whole island looked dead. He saw no one, though he imagined her presence. Freeman thought of tying up at a dock and searching around a bit, but it seemed like folly. Rowing back to Stresa, he was stopped by the lake patrol and compelled to show his passport. An officer advised him not to row on the lake after dark; he might have an accident. The next morning, wearing sunglasses, a light straw, recently purchased, and a seersucker suit, he boarded the vaporetto and soon landed on the island of his dreams, together with the usual group of tourists. But the fanatic guide at once spied Freeman, and waving his cane like a schoolmas-

stationery writing paper, etc.

Re-introducing the motif of name-giving.

serene very content
serenity

intricate complicated

gloomy dark, depressing

folly foolish behaviour

seersucker suit light linen suit with wrinkled surface

ter's rod, called on him to depart peacefully. Fearing a scene that the girl would surely hear of, Freeman left at once, greatly annoyed. The padrona, that night, in a confidential mood, warned him not to have anything to do with anybody on the Isola del Dongo.

The family had a perfidious history and was known for its deceit and trickery.

On Sunday, at the low point of a depression after an afternoon nap, Freeman heard a knock on his door. A long-legged boy in short pants and a torn shirt handed him an envelope, the corner embossed with somebody's coat of arms. Breathlessly, Freeman tore it open and extracted a sheet of thin bluish paper with a few lines of spidery writing on it: "You may come this afternoon at six. Ernesto will accompany you. I. del D."

It was already after five. Freeman was overwhelmed, giddy with pleasure.

"Tu sei Ernesto?" he asked the boy.

The boy, perhaps eleven or twelve, who had been watching Freeman with large curious eyes, shook his head. "No, Signore. Sono Giacobbe."

"Dov'è Ernesto?"

The boy pointed vaguely at the window, which Freeman took to mean that whoever he was was waiting at the lake front.

Freeman changed in the bathroom, emerging in a jiffy with his new straw hat on and the seersucker suit. "Let's go." He ran down the stairs, the boy running after him.

At the dock, to Freeman's startled surprise, "Ernesto" turned out to be the temperamental guide with the pestiferous cane, probably a major domo in the palazzo, long with the family. Now a guide in another context, he was obviously an unwilling one, to judge from his expression. Perhaps a few wise words had subdued him and though haughty still, he settled for a show of politeness. Freeman greeted him courteously. The guide sat not in the ritzy launch Freeman had expected to see, but at the stern of an oversize, weatherbeaten rowboat, a cross between a fishing dory and small lifeboat. Preceded by the boy, Freeman climbed in over the unoccupied part of the rear seat, then, as Giacobbe took his place at the oars, hesitantly sat down next to Ernesto. One of the boatmen on the shore gave them a shove off and the boy began to row. The big boat seemed hard to maneuver, but Giacobbe, working deftly with a pair of long, heavy oars, managed with ease. He rowed quickly from the shore and toward the island where Isabella was waiting.

Freeman, though heartened to be off, contented, loving the wide airy world, wasn't comfortable sitting so snug with Er-

perfidious tending to betray

coat of arms *Wappen*

giddy dizzy

tu sei (It.) are you

sono (It.) I am

dov'è (It.) where is

in a jiffy very quickly

pestiferous dangerous

haughty showing arrogance

ritzy fashionable (derived from *Ritz*, the deluxe hotel)

launch means of transport, boat

hesitant taking (too much) time because one is nervous or worried
to hesitate, hesitation

deftly skilfully

garlic spice, *Knoblauch*
cheroot cigar cut at both ends
slat thin, flat strip
to carouse to drink heavily
hearse vehicle used to transport a dead body in a coffin
greedy wanting to have more
exasperation irritation because sb is frustrated
by dint of using, by means of
to blister *Blasen bekommen*

villain untrustworthy person; criminal
villany, villainous

The traditional image of the typical American. Consider its function in this context.

nesto, who smelled freshly of garlic. The talkative guide was a silent traveller. A dead cheroot hung from the corner of his mouth, and from time to time he absently poked his cane in the slats at the bottom of the boat; if there was no leak, Freeman thought, he would create one. He seemed tired, as if he had been carousing all night and had found no time to rest. Once he removed his black felt hat to mop his head with a handkerchief, and Freeman realized he was bald and looked surprisingly old.

Though tempted to say something pleasant to the old man – no hard feelings on this marvelous journey, Freeman had no idea where to begin. What would he reply to a grunt? After a time of prolonged silence, now a bit on edge, Freeman remarked, "Maybe I'd better row and give the boy a rest?"

"As you weesh." Ernesto shrugged.

Freeman traded places with the boy, then wished he hadn't. The oars were impossibly heavy; he rowed badly, allowing the left oar to sink deeper into the water than the right, thus twisting the boat off course. It was like pulling a hearse, and as he awkwardly splashed the oars around, he was embarrassedly aware of the boy and Ernesto, alike in their dark eyes and greedy beaks, a pair of odd birds, openly staring at him. He wished them far far away from the beautiful island and in exasperation pulled harder. By dint of determined effort, though his palms were painfully blistered, he began to row rhythmically, and the boat went along more smoothly. Freeman gazed up in triumph but they were no longer watching him, the boy trailing a straw in the water, the guide staring dreamily into the distance.

After a while, as if having studied Freeman and decided, when all was said and done, that he wasn't exactly a villain, Ernesto spoke in a not unfriendly tone.

"Everybody says how reech ees America?" he remarked.

"Rich enough," Freeman grunted.

"Also thees ees the same with you?" The guide spoke with a half-embarrassed smile around his drooping cheroot butt.

"I'm comfortable," Freeman replied, and in honesty added, "but I have to work for a living."

"For the young people ees a nice life, no? I mean there ees always what to eat, and for the woman een the house many remarkable machines?"

"Many," Freeman said. Nothing comes from nothing, he thought. He's been asked to ask questions. Freeman then gave the guide an earful on the American standard of living, and he meant living. This for whatever it was worth to such as the

Italian aristocracy. He hoped for the best. You could never tell the needs and desires of others.

Ernesto, as if memorizing what he had just heard, watched Freeman row for a while.

"Are you in biziness?" he ultimately asked.

Freeman searched around and came up with, "Sort of in public relations."

Ernesto now threw away his butt. "Excuse me that I ask. How much does one earn in thees biziness in America?"

Calculating quickly, Freeman replied, "I personally average about a hundred dollars a week. That comes to about a quarter million lire every month."

Ernesto repeated the sum, holding onto his hat in the breeze. The boy's eyes had widened. Freeman hid a satisfied smile.

"And your father?" Here the guide paused, searching Freeman's face.

"What about him?" asked Freeman, tensing.

"What ees hees trade?"

"Was. He's dead – insurance."

Ernesto removed his respectful hat, letting the sunlight bathe his bald head. They said nothing more until they had reached the island, then Freeman, consolidating possible gain, asked him in a complimentary tone where he had learned his English.

"Everywhere," Ernesto replied, with a weary smile, and, Freeman, alert for each shift in prevailing wind, felt that if he hadn't made a bosom friend, he had at least softened an enemy; and that, on home grounds, was going good.

They landed and watched the boy tie up the boat; Freeman asked Ernesto where the signorina was. The guide, now looking bored by it all, pointed his cane at the top terraces, a sweeping gesture that seemed to take in the whole upper half of the luscious island. Freeman hoped the man would not insist on accompanying him and interfering with his meeting with the girl; but when he looked down from looking up without sighting Isabella, both Ernesto and Giacobbe had made themselves scarce. Leave it to the Italians at this sort of thing, Freeman thought.

luscious sweet, seductive

Warning himself to be careful, tactful, he went quickly up the stairs. At each terrace he glanced around, then ran up to the next, his hat already in his hand. He found her, after wandering through profusions of flowers, where he had guessed she would be, alone in the garden behind the palazzo. She was sitting on an old stone bench near a little marble fountain, whose jets from the mouths of mocking elves sparkled in mellow sunlight.

pensive thoughtful
nape the back of the neck
to lope to run easily
indefatigable untiring
elusive hard to grasp, to comprehend
evanescent tending to vanish
transitoriness *Vergänglichkeit*
Explain the emotional ambiguity.
opaque difficult to see through

Beholding her, the lovely face, sharply incised, yet soft in its femininity, the dark eyes pensive, her hair loosely knotted at the nape of her graceful neck, Freeman ached to his oar-blistered fingers. She was wearing a linen blouse of some soft shade of red that fell gently upon her breasts, and a long, slender black skirt; her tanned legs were without stockings; and on her narrow feet she wore sandals. As Freeman approached her, walking slowly to keep from loping, she brushed back a strand of hair, a gesture so beautiful it saddened him, because it was gone in the doing; and though Freeman, on this miraculous Sunday evening was aware of his indefatigable reality, he could not help thinking as he dwelt upon her lost gesture, that she might be as elusive as it, as evanescent; and so might this island be, and so, despite all the days he had lived through, good, bad and boring, that too often sneaked into his thoughts – so, indeed, might he today, tomorrow. He went toward her with a deep sense of the transitoriness of things, but this feeling was overwhelmed by one of pure joy when she rose to give him her hand.

"Welcome," Isabella said, blushing; she seemed happy, yet, in her manner, a little agitated to see him – perhaps one and the same thing – and he wanted then and there to embrace her but could not work up the nerve. Although he felt in her presence a fulfillment, as if they had already confessed love for one another, at the same time Freeman sensed an uneasiness in her which made him think, though he fought the idea, that they were far away from love; or at least were approaching it through opaque mystery. But that's what happened, Freeman, who had often been in love, told himself. Until you were lovers you were strangers.

In conversation he was at first formal. "I thank you for your kind note. I have been looking forward to seeing you."

She turned toward the palazzo. "My people are out. They have gone to a wedding on another island. May I show you something of the palace?"

He was at this news both pleased and disappointed. He did not at the moment feel like meeting her family. Yet if she had presented him, it would have been a good sign.

They walked for a while in the garden, then Isabella took Freeman's hand and led him through a heavy door into the large rococo palazzo.

"What would you care to see?"

Though he had superficially been through two floors of the building, wanting to be led by her, this close to him, Freeman replied, "Whatever you want me to."

She took him first to the chamber where Napoleon had slept. "It wasn't Napoleon himself, who slept here," Isabella explained. "He slept on Isola Bella. His brother Joseph may have been here, or perhaps Pauline, with one of her lovers. No one is sure."

"Oh ho, a trick," said Freeman.

"We often pretend," she remarked. "This is a poor country."

They entered the main picture gallery. Isabella pointed out the Titians, Tintorettos, Bellinis, making Freeman breathless; then at the door of the room she turned with an embarrassed smile and said that most of the paintings in the gallery were copies.

"Copies?" Freeman was shocked.

"Yes, although there are some fair originals from the Lombard school."

"All the Titians are copies?"

"All."

This slightly depressed him. "What about the statuary – also copies?"

"For the most part."

His face fell.

"Is something the matter?"

"Only that I couldn't tell the fake from the real."

"Oh, but many of the copies are exceedingly beautiful," Isabella said. "It would take an expert to tell they weren't originals."

"I guess I've got a lot to learn," Freeman said.

At this she squeezed his hand and he felt better.

But the tapestries, she remarked as they traversed the long hall hung with them, which darkened as the sun set, were genuine and valuable. They meant little to Freeman: long floor-to-ceiling, bluish-green fabrics of woodland scenes: stags, unicorns and tigers disporting themselves, though in one picture, the tiger killed the unicorn. Isabella hurried past this and led Freeman into a room he had not been in before, hung with tapestries of somber scenes from the *Inferno*. One before which they stopped, was of a writhing leper, spotted from head to foot with pustulating sores which he tore at with his nails but the itch went on forever.

"What did he do to deserve his fate?" Freeman inquired.

"He falsely said he could fly."

"For that you go to hell?"

She did not reply. The hall had become gloomily dark, so they left.

From the garden close by the beach where the raft was anchored, they watched the water turn all colors. Isabella had

---

What function does the discussion of art (originals or copies) serve?

fake not original, not true

stag adult male deer

unicorn *Einhorn*

Inferno (It.) hell; here: first part of Dante's *Divine Comedy*

leper *Aussätziger*

pustulating *mit Eiter gefüllt*

sore here: *Aussatz*

What do you know about Icarus? What is the connection to Henry Freeman?

little to say about herself – she seemed to be quite often pensive – and Freeman, concerned with the complexities of the future, though his heart contained multitudes, found himself comparatively silent. When the night was complete, as the moon was rising, Isabella said she would be gone for a moment, and stepped behind a shrub. When she came forth, Freeman had this utterly amazing vision of her, naked, but before he could even focus his eyes on her flowerlike behind, she was already in the water, swimming for the raft. After an anguished consideration of could he swim that far or would he drown, Freeman, eager to see her from up close (she was sitting on the raft, showing her breasts to the moon) shed his clothes behind the shrub where her delicate things lay, and walked down the stone steps into the warm water. He swam awkwardly, hating the picture he must make in her eyes, Apollo Belvedere slightly maimed; and still suffered visions of drowning in twelve feet of water. Or suppose she had to jump in to rescue him? However, nothing risked, nothing gained, so he splashed on and made the raft with breath to spare, his worries always greater than their cause.

Apollo Belvedere famous sculpture
to maim to injure

But when he had pulled himself up on the raft, to his dismay, Isabella was no longer there. He caught a glimpse of her on the shore, darting behind the shrub. Nursing gloomy thoughts, Freeman rested a while, then, when he had sneezed twice and presupposed a nasty cold, jumped into the water and splashed his way back to the island. Isabella, already clothed, was waiting with a towel. She threw it to Freeman as he came up the steps, and withdrew while he dried himself and dressed. When he came forth in his seersucker, she offered salami, prosciutto, cheese, bread, and red wine, from a large platter delivered from the kitchen. Freeman, for a while angered at the runaround on the raft, relaxed with the wine and feeling of freshness after a bath. The mosquitoes behaved long enough for him to say he loved her. Isabella kissed him tenderly, then Ernesto and Giacobbe appeared and rowed him back to Stresa.

to dart to move quickly

Monday morning Freeman didn't know what to do with himself. He awoke with restless memories, enormously potent, many satisfying, some burdensome; they ate him, he ate them. He felt he should somehow have made every minute with her better, hadn't begun to say half of what he had wanted – the kind of man he was, what they could get out of life together. And he regretted that he hadn't gotten quickly to the raft, still excited by what might have happened if he had reached it before she had left. But a memory was only a memory – you could forget, not change it. On the other hand,

burdensome difficult to bear

he was pleased, surprised by what he had accomplished: the evening alone with her, the trusting, intimate sight of her beautiful body, her kiss, the unspoken promise of love. His desire for her was so splendid it hurt. He wandered through the afternoon, dreaming of her, staring often at the glittering islands in the opaque lake. By nightfall he was exhausted and went to sleep oppressed by all he had lived through.

It was strange, he thought, as he lay in bed waiting to sleep, that of all his buzzing worries he was worried most about one. If Isabella loved him, as he now felt she did or would before very long; with the strength of this love they could conquer their problems as they arose. He anticipated a good handful, stirred up, in all probability, by her family; but life in the U.S.A. was considered by many Italians, including aristocrats (else why had Ernesto been sent to sniff out conditions there?) a fine thing for their marriageable daughters. Given this additional advantage, things would somehow get worked out, especially if Isabella, an independent girl, gazed a little eagerly at the star-spangled shore. Her family would give before flight in her eyes. No, the worry that troubled him most was the lie he had told her, that he wasn't a Jew. He could, of course, confess, say she knew Levin, not Freeman, man of adventure, but that might ruin all, since it was quite clear she wanted nothing to do with a Jew, or why, at first sight, had she asked so searching a question? Or he might admit nothing and let her, more or less, find out after she had lived a while in the States and seen it was no crime to be Jewish; that a man's past was, it could safely be said, expendable. Yet this treatment, if the surprise was upsetting, might cause recriminations later on. Another solution might be one he had thought of often: to change his name (he had considered Le Vin but preferred Freeman) and forget he had ever been born Jewish. There was no question of hurting family, or being embarrassed by them, he the only son of both parents dead. Cousins lived in Toledo, Ohio, where they would always live and never bother. And when he brought Isabella to America they could skip N.Y.C. and go to live in a place like San Francisco, where nobody knew him and nobody "would know." To arrange such details and prepare other minor changes was why he figured on a trip or two home before they were married; he was prepared for that. As for the wedding itself, since he would have to marry her here to get her out of Italy, it would probably have to be in a church, but he would go along with that to hasten things. It was done everyday. Thus he decided, although it did not entirely satisfy him; not

➔ Why does it trouble him?

expendable here: able to be neglected

recrimination a charge against the accuser

crime, criminal, to discriminate against, discriminating

➔ The central motif of name change again.

➔ Analyse his conflict.

denial refusal to accept

so much the denial of being Jewish – what had it brought him but headaches, inferiorities, unhappy memories? – as the lie to the beloved. At first sight love and a lie; it lay on his heart like a sore. Yet, if that was the way it had to be, it was the way.

let alone *geschweige denn*

He awoke the next morning, beset by a swarm of doubts concerning his plans and possibilities. When would he see Isabella again, let alone marry her? ("When?" he had whispered before getting into the boat, and she had vaguely promised, "Soon.") Soon was brutally endless. The mail brought nothing and Freeman grew dismayed.

to seduce here: to call for

Cupid Roman god of love

Had he, he asked himself, been constructing a hopeless fantasy, wish seducing probability? Was he inventing a situation that didn't exist, namely, her feeling for him, the possibility of a future with her? He was desperately casting about for something to keep his mood from turning dark blue, when a knock sounded on his door. The padrona, he thought, because she often came up for one unimportant thing or another, but to his unspeakable joy it was Cupid in short pants – Giacobbe holding forth the familiar envelope. She would meet him, Isabella wrote, at two o'clock in the piazza where the electric tram took off for Mt. Mottarone, from whose summit one saw the beautiful panorama of lakes and mountains in the region. Would he share this with her?

to quash to crush or repress

The difference between ➲ "elope" and "flee", p. 9.

to elope to run away
to savor to enjoy or appreciate a taste or experience

Although he had quashed the morning's anxiety, Freeman was there at one P.M., smoking impatiently. His sun rose as she appeared, but as she came towards him he noticed she was not quite looking at him (in the distance he could see Giacobbe rowing away) her face neutral, inexpressive. He was at first concerned, but she had, after all, written the letter to him, so he wondered what hot nails she had had to walk on to get off the island. He must sometime during the day drop the word "elope" to see if she savored it. But whatever was bothering her, Isabella immediately shook off. She smiled as she greeted him; he hoped for her lips but got instead her polite fingers. These he kissed in broad daylight (let the spies tell papa) and she shyly withdrew her hand. She was wearing – it surprised him, though he gave her credit for resisting foolish pressures – exactly the same blouse and skirt she had worn on Sunday. They boarded the tram with a dozen tourists and sat alone on the open seat in front; as a reward for managing this she permitted Freeman to hold her hand. He sighed. The tram, drawn by an old electric locomotive moved slowly through the town and more slowly up the slope of the mountain.

They rode for close to two hours, watching the lake fall as the mountains rose. Isabella, apart from pointing to something now and then, was again silent, withdrawn, but Freeman, allowing her her own rate at flowering, for the moment without plans, was practically contented. A long vote for an endless journey; but the tram at last came to a stop and they walked through a field thick with wildflowers, up the slope to the summit of the mountain. Though the tourists followed in a crowd, the mountain top was broad and they stood near its edge, to all intents and purposes alone. Below them, on the green undulating plains of Piedmont and Lombardy, seven lakes were scattered, each a mirror reflecting whose fate? And high in the distance rose a ring of astonishing snow-clad Alps. Ah, he murmured, and fell silent.

"We say here," Isabella said, "'un pezzo di paradiso caduto dal cielo.'"

"You can say it again." Freeman was deeply moved by the sublimity of the distant Alps. She named the white peaks from Mt. Rosa to the Jungfrau. Gazing at them, he felt he had grown a head taller and was inspired to accomplish a feat men would wonder at.

"Isabella –" Freeman turned to ask her to marry him; but she was standing apart from him, her face pale.

Pointing to the snowy mountains, her hand moving in a gentle arc, she asked, "Don't those peaks – those seven – look like a Menorah?"

"Like a what?" Freeman politely inquired. He had a sudden frightening remembrance of her seeing him naked as he came out of the lake and felt constrained to tell her that circumcision was de rigueur in stateside hospitals; but he didn't dare. She may not have noticed.

"Like a seven-branched candalabrum holding white candles in the sky?" Isabella asked.

"Something like that."

"Or do you see the Virgin's crown adorned with jewels?"

"Maybe the crown," he faltered. "It all depends how you look at it."

They left the mountain and went down to the water. The tram ride was faster going down. At the lake front, as they were waiting for Giacobbe to come with the rowboat, Isabella, her eyes troubled, told Freeman she had a confession to make. He, still eager to propose, hoped she would finally say she loved him. Instead, she said, "My name is not del Dongo. It is Isabella della Seta. The del Dongos have not been on the island in years. We are the caretakers of the palace, my father, brother and I. We are poor people."

"Caretakers?" Freeman was astonished.

undulating wavy

clad covered in

un pezzo di paradiso caduto dal cielo (It.) a piece of paradise has fallen from heaven

feat an act of courage

The different religious symbolism of Menorah and Virgin's Crown.

Menorah candalabrum with seven branches used in Jewish worship

circumcision *Beschneidung*

de rigueur (Fr.) obligatory

Virgin's Crown symbol of Christianity

to falter to stammer

to propose to suggest, here: to ask sb to marry you
proposal, proposition

Freeman's gradual disappointment as a prelude to his final disillusionment.

"Yes."

"Ernesto is your father?" His voice rose.

She nodded.

"Was it his idea for you to say you were somebody else?"

"No, mine. He did what I asked him to. He has wanted me to go to America, but under the right circumstances."

"So you had to pretend," he said bitterly. He was more greatly disturbed than he could account for, as if he had been expecting just this to happen.

She blushed and turned away. "I was not sure of the circumstances. I wanted you to stay until I knew you better."

"Why didn't you say so?"

"Perhaps I wasn't serious in the beginning. I said what I thought you wanted to hear. At the same time I wished you to stay. I thought you would be clearer to me after a while."

"Clearer how?"

"I don't really know." Her eyes searched his, then she dropped her glance.

"I'm not hiding anything," he said. He wanted to say more but warned himself not to.

"That's what I was afraid of."

peas in a pod people who are very similar in appearance

Giacobbe had come with the boat and steadied it for his sister. They were alike as the proverbial peas – two dark Italian faces, the Middle Ages looking out of their eyes. Isabella got into the boat and Giacobbe pushed off with one oar. She waved from afar.

to irk to cause pain or irritation

Outline his self-imposed mental and emotional confusion.

Freeman went back to bis pensione in a turmoil, hurt where it hurts – in his dreams, thinking he should have noticed before how worn her blouse and skirt were, should have seen more than he had. It was this that irked. He called himself a damn fool for making up fairy tales – Freeman in love with the Italian aristocracy. He thought of taking off for Venice or Florence, but bis heart ached for love of her, and he could not forget that he had originally come in the simple hope of finding a girl worth marrying. If the desire had developed complications, the fault was mostly his own. After an hour in his room, burdened by an overpowering loneliness, Freeman felt he must have her. She mustn't get away from him. So what if the countess had become a caretaker? She was a natural-born queen, whether by del Dongo or any other name. So she had lied to him, but so had he to her; they were quits on that score and his conscience was calm. He felt things would be easier all around now that the air had been cleared.

Freeman ran down to the dock; the sun had set and the boatmen were home, swallowing spaghetti. He was considering untying one of the rowboats and paying tomorrow, when he caught sight of someone sitting on a bench – Ernesto, in his hot winter hat, smoking a cheroot.

He was resting his wrists on the handle of his cane, his chin on them.

"You weesh a boat?" the guide asked in a not unkindly tone.

"With all my heart. Did Isabella send you?"

"No."

He came because she was unhappy, Freeman guessed – maybe crying. There's a father for you, a real magician despite his appearance. He waves his stick and up pops Freeman for his little girl.

"Get een," said Ernesto.

"I'll row," said Freeman. He had almost added "father," but had caught himself. As if guessing the jest, Ernesto smiled, a little sadly. But he sat at the stern of the boat, enjoying the ride.

jest *Scherz, Spaß*

In the middle of the lake, seeing the mountains surrounding it lit in the last glow of daylight, Freeman thought of the "Menorah" in the Alps. Where had she got the word, he wondered, and decided anywhere, a book or picture. But wherever she had, he must settle this subject once and for all tonight.

When the boat touched the dock, the pale moon rose. Ernesto tied up, and handed Freeman a flashlight.

"Een the jarden," he said tiredly, pointing with his cane.

"Don't wait up." Freeman hastened to the garden at the lake's edge, where the roots of trees hung like hoary beards above the water; the flashlight didn't work, but the moon and his memory were enough. Isabella, God bless her, was standing at the low wall among the moonlit statuary: stags, tigers and unicorns, poets and painters, shepherds with pipes, and playful shepherdesses, gazing at the light shimmering on the water.

hoary grey-haired

She was wearing white, the figure of a future bride; perhaps it was an altered wedding dress – he would not be surprised if a hand-me-down, the way they saved clothes in this poor country. He had pleasant thoughts of buying her some nifty outfits.

She was motionless, her back toward him – though he could picture her bosom breathing. When he said good evening, lifting his light straw, she turned to him with a sweet smile. He tenderly kissed her lips; this she let him do, softly returning the same.

"Goodbye," Isabella whispered.

"To whom goodbye?" Freeman affectionately mocked. "I have come to marry you."

Sketch Freeman's final and utter failure.

She gazed at him with eyes moistly bright, then came the soft, inevitable thunder: "Are you a Jew?"

"Why should I lie?" he thought; she's mine for the asking. But then he trembled with the fear of at the last moment losing her, so Freeman answered, though his scalp prickled, "How many no's make never? Why do you persist with such foolish questions?"

"Because I hoped you were." Slowly she unbuttoned her bodice, arousing Freeman, though he was thoroughly confused as to her intent. When she revealed her breasts – he could have wept at their beauty (now recalling a former invitation to gaze at them, but he had arrived too late on the raft) – to his horror he discerned tatooed on the soft and tender flesh a bluish line of distorted numbers.

to distort to twist out of proportion
Buchenwald concentration camp in Nazi-ruled Weimar
to incense to make angry
to stun to shock sb senseless
desecration destruction of sth sacred

"Buchenwald," Isabella said, "when I was a little girl. The Fascists sent us there. The Nazis did it."

Freeman groaned, incensed at the cruelty, stunned by the desecration.

"I can't marry you. We are Jews. My past is meaningful to me. I treasure what I suffered for."

"Jews," he muttered, "– you? Oh, God, why did you keep this from me, too?"

"I did not wish to tell you something you would not welcome. I thought at one time it was possible you were – I hoped but was wrong."

"Isabella –" he cried brokenly. "Listen, I – I am –"

He groped for her breasts, to clutch, kiss or suckle them; but she had stepped among the statues, and when he vainly sought her in the veiled mist that had risen from the lake, still calling her name, Freeman embraced only moonlit stone.

Multi-ethnicity in the English-speaking world

A nation of immigrants: Multi-ethnicity in the United States

It was their land: The Native Americans

Michael Blake, Dances with Wolves

Michael Blake's novel and, even more so, Kevin Costner's film-version in 1992 moved millions with the inter-cultural love affair between Lieutenant John Dunbar and the Comanche woman (a white woman by birth) Stands With a Fist who meet in the West of 1863. Dunbar befriends a wolf (hence the title of the novel) and makes friends with the Comanche almost to the point of becoming a Comanche himself. He feels compelled to mediate between the world of the Indians and that of the white soldiers and settlers. Before the white army moves in, he leaves his Indian friends and flees with his wife and their baby.

one

In a quiet way it was one of the most satisfying days of Lieutenant Dunbar's life.

Kicking Bird's family greeted him with a warmth and respect that made him feel like more than a guest. They were genuinely happy to see him.

He and Kicking Bird settled down for a smoke that, because of constant but pleasant interruptions, lasted well into the afternoon.

Word of Lieutenant Dunbar's name and how he got it spread through camp with the usual astonishing speed, and any nagging suspicions the people might have harbored toward the white soldier evaporated with this inspiring news.

What does the reader get to know about the social life of the Comanche? Collect telling examples.

nagging annoying, troubling

suspicion mistrust, strong doubt
to suspect, suspicious

He was not a god, but neither was he like any hair mouth they had encountered. He was a man of medicine. Warriors dropped by constantly, some of them wanting to say hello, others wanting nothing more than to lay eyes on Dances With Wolves.

The lieutenant recognized most of them now. At each arrival he would stand and make his short bow. Some of them bowed back. A few extended their hands, as they had seen him do.

to rehash to go over again

There wasn't much they could talk about, but the lieutenant was getting good with signs, good enough to rehash some of the recent hunt's high points. This formed the basis for most of the visiting.

After a couple of hours the steady stream of visitors trickled away to no one, and Dunbar was just wondering why he hadn't seen Stands With A Fist, and if she was on the agenda, when Wind In His Hair suddenly walked in.

Before greetings could be exchanged, each man's attention was drawn to the items they had traded: the unbuttoned tunic and the gleaming breastplate. For both of them it was a subtly reassuring sight.

As they shook hands Lieutenant Dunbar thought, I like this fellow; it's good to see him.

The same sentiments were foremost in Wind In His Hair's thoughts, and they sat down together for an amicable chat, though neither man could understand what the other was saying.

pemmican dried meat

Kicking Bird called to his wife for food, and the trio soon devoured a lunch of pemmican and berries. They ate without saying a word.

to divine to guess, to speculate
divine, divinity

After the meal another pipe was packed and the two Indians fell into a conversation that the lieutenant could not divine. By their gestures and speech, however he guessed they were dealing with something beyond idle chitchat.

They seemed to be planning some activity, and he was not surprised when, at the end of their talk, both men stood up and asked him to follow as they went outside.

cache hiding place

Dunbar trailed them to the rear of Kicking Bird's tepee, where a cache of material was waiting for them. A neat stack of limber willow poles was sitting next to a high pile of dried brush.

arbor *Laube*

The two men had another, even briefer discussion, then set to work. When the lieutenant saw what was taking shape, he lent a hand here and there, but before he could contribute much, the material had been transformed into a shady arbor four or five feet high.

A small portion had been left uncovered to afford an entrance, and Lieutenant Dunbar was shown inside first. There wasn't enough room to stand up, but once he was down, he found the place roomy and peaceful. The brush made good cover against the sun and was sheer enough to allow for a free flow of air. It wasn't until he'd finished this quick inspection that he realized Kicking Bird and Wind In His Hair had vanished. A week ago he would have been uncomfortable with their sudden desertion. But, like the Indians, he was no longer suspicious. The lieutenant was content to sit quietly against the surprisingly strong back wall, listening to the now familiar sounds of Ten Bears's camp as he awaited developments.

They were not long in coming.

Only a few minutes had passed before he heard footsteps approaching. Kicking Bird duck-walked through the entrance and seated himself far enough away to leave a full space between them.

A shadow falling across the entrance told Dunbar that someone else was waiting to come inside. Without thinking, he assumed it was Wind In His Hair.

Kicking Bird called out softly. The shadow shifted to the accompaniment of tinkling bells, and Stands With A Fist stooped through the doorway.

Dunbar scooted to one side, making room as she maneuvered between them, and in the few seconds it took her to settle, he saw much that was new.

The bells were sewn on the sides of finely beaded moccasins. Her doeskin dress looked like an heirloom, something well cared for and not for every day. The bodice was sprinkled with small, thick bones arranged in rows. They were elk's teeth. The wrist closest to him wore a bracelet of solid brass. Around her neck was a choker of the same pipe-bone he wore on his chest. Her hair, fresh and fragrant, hung down her back in a single braid, exposing more of the high-cheeked, distinctly browed face than he had seen before. She looked more delicate and feminine to him now. And more white.

It dawned on the lieutenant then that the arbor had been built as a place for them to meet. And in the time it took her to sit, he realized how much he had anticipated seeing her again.

She still wouldn't look at him, and while Kicking Bird mumbled something to her, he made up his mind to take the initiative and say hello.

It so happened that they turned their heads, opened their mouths, and said the word at precisely the same time. The two hellos collided in the space between them, and the speakers recoiled awkwardly at their accidental beginning.

sheer very thin

➊ Trace the stages of the beginning love.

to stoop to bow

doeskin made of female deer skin
heirloom sth left or given by ancestor
bracelet ornamental band worn round the wrist
choker necklace that fits tightly round the neck
braid *Zopf*

omen sign indicating the future

Kicking Bird saw a favourable omen in the accident. He saw two people of like mind. Because this was exactly what he hoped for, it struck him as ironic.

The medicine man chuckled to himself. Then he pointed to Lieutenant Dunbar and grunted, as if saying, "Go ahead ... you first."

"Hello," he said pleasantly.

She lifted her head. Her expression was businesslike, but he could see nothing of the hostility that had been there before.

"Hulo," she replied.

two

They sat a long time in the arbor that day, most of it spent reviewing the few simple words they had exchanged at their first formal session.

Toward sundown, when all three had wearied of the constant, stumbling repetitions, the English translation for her Indian name suddenly came to Stands With A Fist.

It so excited her that she began immediately to teach it to Lieutenant Dunbar. First she had to get across what she wanted. She pointed to him and said, "Jun," then pointed to herself and said nothing. In the same motion she held up a finger that said, "Stop. I will show you."

The pattern had been for him to perform whatever action she asked for, then guess the action's word in English. She wanted him to stand, but that was impossible in the arbor, so she hustled both men outside, where they would have full freedom of movement.

Lieutenant Dunbar guessed "rise," "rises," "gets up," and "on my feet" before he hit "stands." "With" was not so hard, "a" had already been covered, and he got "fist" on the first try.

After he had it in English, she taught him the Comanche.

From there, in rapid succession, he mastered Wind In His Hair, Ten Bears, and Kicking Bird.

sliver small slice

Lieutenant Dunbar was excited. He asked for something to make marks, and using a sliver of charcoal, he wrote the four names in phonetic Comanche on a strip of thin, white bark.

spark quick flash of bright light

Interpret the images used to show the power of language in communication.

Stands With A Fist kept her reserve throughout. But inwardly she was thrilled. The English words were showering in her head like sparks as thousands of doors, locked up for so long, swung open. She was delirious with the excitement of learning.

Each time the lieutenant ran down the list written on his scrap of bark and each time he came close to pronouncing the names as they should be pronounced, she encouraged him with the suggestion of a smile and said the word "yes." For his part, Lieutenant Dunbar did not have to see her little smile to know that the encouragement was heartfelt. He could hear it in the sound of the word and he could see it in the power of her pale brown eyes. To hear him say these words, in English and Comanche, meant something special to her. Her inward thrill was tingling all about them. The lieutenant could feel it.

She was not the same woman, so sad and lost, that he had found on the prairie. That moment was now something left behind. It made him happy to see how far she had come.

Best of all was the little piece of bark he held in his hands. He grasped it firmly, determined not to let it slip away. It was the first section of a map that would guide him into whatever future he had with these people. So many things would be possible from now on.

It was Kicking Bird, however, who was most profoundly affected by this turn of events. To him it was a miracle of the highest order, on a par with attending something all-consuming, like birth or death.

His dream had become reality.

When he heard the lieutenant say his name in Comanche, it was as though an impenetrable wall had suddenly turned to smoke. And they were walking through. They were communicating.

With equal force his view of Stands With A Fist had enlarged. She was no longer a Comanche. In making herself a bridge for their words, she had become something more. Like the lieutenant, he heard it in the sound of her English words and he saw it in the new power of her eyes. Something had been added, something that was missing before, and Kicking Bird knew what it was.

Her long-buried blood was running again, her undiluted white blood.

The impact of these things was more than even Kicking Bird could bear, and like a professor who knows when it is time for his pupils to take a rest, he told Stands With A Fist that this was enough for one day.

A trace of disappointment flashed on her face. Then she dropped her head and nodded submissively.

At that moment, however, a wonderful thought occurred to her. She caught Kicking Bird's eye and respectfully asked if they might do one more thing.

She wanted to teach the white soldier his name.

Explain how the image of the wall and of the bridge are represented in this context.

impenetrable incapable of being penetrated or pierced

undiluted not thinned or watered down

It was a good idea, so good that Kicking Bird could not refuse his adopted daughter. He told her to continue.

She remembered the word right away. She could see it, but she couldn't speak it. And she couldn't remember how she had done it as a girl. The men waited while she tried to remember.

Then Lieutenant Dunbar unwittingly raised his hand to brush at a gnat that was bothering his ear, and she saw it all again. She grabbed the lieutenant's hand as it hung in space and let the fingertips of her other hand rest cautiously on his hip. And before either man could react, she led Dunbar into a creaky but unmistakable memory of a waltz.

gnat small biting fly

After a few seconds she pulled away demurely, leaving Lieutenant Dunbar in a state of shock. He had to struggle to remember the point of the exercise.

demure modest, reserved

A light went off in his head. Then it jumped into his eyes, and like the only boy in class who knows the answer, he smiled at his teacher.

three

From there it was easy to get the rest.

Lieutenant Dunbar went to one knee and wrote the name at the bottom of his bark grammar book. His eyes lingered on the way it looked in English. It seemed bigger than just a name. The more he looked at it, the more he liked it.

He said it to himself. Dances With Wolves.

The lieutenant came to his feet, bowed shortly in Kicking Bird's direction, and, as a butler might announce the arrival of a dinner guest, humbly and without fanfare, he said the name once more.

What does this signify? ➔

This time he said it in Comanche.

"Dances With Wolves."

Buffy Sainte-Marie, Now that the Buffalo's Gone

Though quite prominent as an artist and educator, Buffy Sainte-Marie, a member of the First Nation, is best remembered as a political and environmental activist and a protest singer who at the height of the protest movement in the sixties and seventies lent a voice to the problems of the Native Americans. As in the following song she put the suffering of her people in a global context of human suffering and dignity.

Can you remember the times
That you have held your head high
and told all your friends of your Indian claim
Proud good lady and proud good man
Some great great grandfather from Indian blood came
and you feel in your heart for these ones

Oh it's written in books and in song
that we've been mistreated and wronged
Well over and over I hear those same words
from you good lady and you good man
Well listen to me if you care where we stand
and you feel you're a part of these ones

When a war between nations is lost
the loser we know pays the cost
but even when Germany fell to your hands
consider dear lady, consider dear man
you left them their pride and you left them their land
and what have you done to these ones

Has a change come about my dear man
or are you still taking our lands
A treaty forever your senators sign
They do dear lady, they do dear man
and the treaties are broken again and again
and what will you do for these ones

Oh it's all in the past you can say
but it's still going on here today
The governments now want the Navaho land
that of the Inuit and the Cheyenne
It's here and it's now you can help us dear man
Now that the buffalo's gone.

The singer puts the treatment of her fellow Indians and the extinction of the buffalo into the wider context of discrimination and war. What does she refer to with the words "the buffalo's gone"?

Look for further information on the American Indian tribes mentioned here. Explain the term currently used for them: First Nations.

Simon J. Ortiz, The Killing of a State Cop

The story is told from the point of view of an adult recalling and reflecting on a decisive experience in his life. The frame reveals the narrator's attitude towards the main character and his crime. Felipe is largely the victim of a pecking-order among the minorities in which the American Indian keeps a position below the Latinos and of a discrimination which has hurt his self-esteem.

trough open box for animals to feed or drink from

What do we get to know about Felipe prior to his crime?

Felipe was telling me how it happened. I was then twelve years old. They would get him, he knew, he said. And he was scared. He looked around nervously all the time that we sat on the trough which ran around the water tank.

Felipe wasn't a bad guy. Not at all. A little wild maybe. He had been in the marines and he could have gotten kicked out if he had wanted to, he said. But he hadn't because he could play it pretty straight like a good guy, too.

He used to tell me a lot of things, about what he had seen, about what he had done, about what he planned to do, and about what other people could do to you. That was one trouble with him. He was always thinking about what other people could do to you. Not the people around our place, the Indians, but other people.

How that state policeman died was like this (Felipe wanted me to remember what he said always, and he talked very seriously and sometimes sadly, and again he said they would get him anyway):

"What the hell. He deserved to die, the bastard."

It was the wine, Felipe said. And that thing he had about people, I guess. He didn't say, but I knew.

"It makes you warm in the head and other things like that," he said.

bootlegger person illegally selling alcohol

He had gone to town from the reservation with Antonio, his brother. They drove their pickup truck to town where they bought the wine from a bootlegger. "From some stupid Mexican bartender. Geesus, I hate Mexicans."

Felipe spat on the ground. Indians were not supposed to drink or buy liquor at that time. It was against the law. Felipe hated the law and broke it whenever he felt he could get away with it.

depot (AE) railway station

to pee to urinate

"One time in Winslow I got off the train when it stopped at the depot and walked into a bar next to the depot to buy a beer. I was still in the marines then and in uniform. This barman, he looked at me very mean and asked if I was Indian. 'Shore,' I said. And he told me to get the hell out before he called the cops. Goddamn. I hated that, and I went around the back and peed on the back door. I don't know why, just because I hated him, I guess."

The scenery of the story changes from town to highway and reservation? To what effect?

Felipe and his brother were walking in town, not saying anything much, and maybe looking at things they wanted to buy when they had the money. They stopped in front of the Golden Theater and looked at the pictures of what was in the movies that day and the next day.

"Hey, Indio. Hey, what hell you doing?" It was Luis Baca, a

member of the state police who patrolled the state highway near the reservation.

The brothers hated the man. Felipe regarded him with a fierce hate because he had been thrown in jail by him once. He had been beaten, and he feared the cop because of that. They did not answer.

"Hey, goddammey Indio, get the hell away from there. Get out of town."

For no reason at all.

"For no reason at all. Goddamn, I got mad and I called him a dirty, fat, lazy good-for-nothing, ugly Mexican."

Felipe looked around him and told me I better learn to be something more than him, a guy who would probably die in the electric chair up at Santa Fe.

Felipe told Antonio he was going to kill the Mexican, but Antonio said that it was no good talk and persuaded him to leave town.

They left, followed by the curses and jeers of Luis Baca. When they got back to the pickup truck, they opened another bottle of wine and drank.

"It makes a noise in your head, and you want to do something," Felipe told me.

They decided to go home. Almost out of town, they heard a siren scream behind them and saw a black police car with Baca driving it. Felipe told Antonio not to stop. They did not go faster, though. Luis Baca drove alongside and laughed at the brothers, who were frightened and suspicious.

Antonio stepped on the brake then, and he let the policeman pass them. They were past the town limits.

"Antonio, my brother, he is a kind of a funny guy," Felipe said. "He doesn't get mad like me. I mean yell or cuss. He just kind of looks mean or sad. He told me to give him the wine and he drank some and put it on the seat between his legs."

The police car leading and pickup truck following were heading toward the reservation.

Suddenly, a few miles out of town, Antonio pressed his foot down on the gas pedal and the pickup truck picked up speed. It seemed that the policeman did not see the truck bearing down on him until it was almost too late.

"Antonio wasn't trying to run into the car. I thought he was going to, but he was only trying to scare the bastard."

Luis Baca swerved off the road anyway, and there was a cloud of dust as his car skidded into a shallow ditch.

Felipe and Antonio didn't stop. Looking through the rear

fierce violent, cruel

curses, jeers nasty and insulting comments

❶ What does the metaphor of the chase underline? What does the excessive brutality illustrate?

suspicious mistrustful

brake mechanism for reducing speed

to cuss to use violent language

mean nasty

to bear down on to move towards threateningly

to swerve to change direction suddenly

to skid (of a car) to slip sideways

shallow not deep

window, they saw the cop get out of the car. Antonio stopped the pickup truck. He started up again and made a U-turn. Passing by the police car, they saw that the policeman was trying to get his car out. The tires kept spinning and throwing gravel. A few miles down the road, they turned around and headed back toward the police car again.

to spin to move round rapidly
gravel small stones mixed with sand

"Wine makes you do stupid things. Son-of-a-bitch. Sometimes you think about putting your hand between a girl's legs or taking money from somebody or even killing somebody."

They slowed down as they approached the police car. It was slowly coming out of the ditch.

ditch *Straßengraben*

"I drank the wine left in the bottle, and as we passed I threw the bottle against the window of the car and I made a dirty sign with my hand at the Mexican," Felipe said.

Antonio speeded the truck up. They kept looking back, and soon they saw the police car following them and heard the siren. They turned into the road that led into the reservation. It was a dirt road, and the truck bounced and jolted as they sped along it. The police car turned off the highway and followed them.

to bounce to jump back
to jolt to move along with bumps

Felipe reached behind the seat of the truck and brought out a 30–30 Winchester rifle which was wrapped in a homemade case of denim from old Levis. He took the rifle out of the denim case and pulled down the lever so that the chamber was open. There was nothing in there, and he closed the lever and lowered the hammer very carefully as usual. He opened the truck compartment and brought out an almost full box of cartridges.

denim cotton cloth
lever *Hebel zum Laden und Spannen*
chamber, hammer *Kammer, Hahn*
cartridge *Patrone*

"You remember that 30–30 I was using when I went deer hunting last year? The one I let you shoot even though you aren't supposed to before you shoot at a deer with it. That one. My father bought it when he was working for the railroad. That one."

They followed the road that led to the village, but turned off to another road before they got there. The road climbed a hill and led toward Black Mesa, several miles to the south. At the top of the hill they stopped and watched to see if the police car was still following them. It was at the bottom of the hill and coming up.

The dirt road led through a forest of juniper and piñon. This was near the heart of the reservation. They sped by a scattered herd of sheep tended by a boy who looked at them as they passed by. The sheep dogs barked at them and ran alongside for a while.

juniper *amerik. Lärche*
piñon *(Span.) Pinie*
to scatter to go off in different directions
to tend to watch over

"The road is very rough and sometimes sandy, and we couldn't go too fast. No one uses it except sheepherders and people going for wood in their wagons. We stopped on a small hill to see if Luis Baca was still coming after us. We couldn't see him because of the forest, so I told my brother to shut off the engine so I could listen. It was real quiet in the forest like it always is, and you can hear things from a long ways away. I could hear the cop car still coming, about a half-mile back. I told Antonio to go on."

They passed the windmill which was a mile from Black Mesa. The one road branched there into several directions. The one that led east of Black Mesa into some rough country and canyons was the one they chose.

Antonio slowed the truck and drove slowly until they saw that the policeman could see which road they had taken, and then he speeded up again.

"Aiee, I can see stupidity in a man. Sometimes even my own. I can see a man's drunkenness making him do crazy things. And Luis Baca, a very stupid son-of-a-bitch, was more than I could see. He wanted to die. And I, because I was drunken and *muy loco* like a Mexican friend I had from Nogales used to say about me when we would play with the whores in Korea and Tokyo, wanted to make him die. I did not care for anything else except that Luis Baca who I hated was going to die."

Directly to the east of Black Mesa is a plain which runs for about two miles in all directions. There is grass on the plain, and there are many prairie dogs. At the edge of the grassy plain is a thin forest of juniper and piñon. A few yards beyond the edge of the forest there is a deep ravine which is the tail end of a deep and wide canyon which runs from the east toward Black Mesa. The ravine comes to a point almost against one edge of Black Mesa. There is only a narrow passage, which crumbles away each year with erosion, between the ravine and the abruptly rising slopes of the mesa. The road passes this point and goes around the mesa and to a spring called Spider Spring.

The brothers passed through the narrow passage and stopped fifty yards away. Felipe got out with the rifle and bullets, and Antonio parked the pickup truck behind a growth of stunted juniper growing thickly together.

"I took some bullets out of the box and put them into the rifle. Six of them, I think, the kind with soft points. I laid down the rifle for a while and waited for Antonio. He didn't come right away from the truck and I called to him. We laid down behind a small mound of sand and rocks; the ground was hot from the sun. We could hear the police car coming.

muy loco (Span.) quite crazy

whore (old-fashioned) prostitute

ravine deep, narrow valley

tail end very end

slope area of rising or falling ground

to stunt to hinder the normal growth

"'Are we just going to scare him so he won't bother us no more?' Antonio asked me.

"I looked at Antonio, and he looked like he used to when we were kids and he used to pretend not to be scared of rattle-snakes.

"'I don't know,' I said. I was going to shoot the man. I don't know why, but I was going to. Maybe I was kind of scared then.

"When the car came out of the trees, it was not coming very fast. It approached the narrow place and slowed down. I thought Luis Baca would see me, so I slid down until I could barely see over the edge of the mound behind which we lay.

mound small hill

"He had slowed down because of the narrow place, and I thought he would stop and turn back. But he didn't. He shifted into first and came on very slowly. That's when I put my rifle on a flat rock and aimed it. Right at the windshield where the steering wheel is. The sun was shining on the windshield very brightly and I could not see very well."

Explain what the violence in this scene is meant to express.

Felipe relaxed a bit, took a breath, opened and closed the lever on the rifle.

lever *Hebel*

The bullet made a hole right above where the metal and glass were joined by a strip of rubber in front of the steering wheel. It made an irregular pattern in the windshield glass. The shot echoed back and forth in the ravine and was followed by another shot. The bullet made a hole a few inches to the upper right of the first. Another shot followed and it was wild. It ricocheted off the top and into some rocks on the mesa slope.

to ricochet (of a shot) to skip or bounce off

"Four times I shot, and I could see the holes almost in the spot where I wanted them to be. One wasn't though. But the car didn't stop or go crooked. It kept coming and crossed the narrow place. It stopped then, and Luis Baca got out very slowly. He called something like he was crying. *'Compadre,'* he said. He held up his right hand and reached to us. There was blood on his neck and shoulder."

compadre (Span.) friend, buddy

Felipe settled himself into place and aimed very carefully. Luis Baca tried to unbuckle his pistol belt, but the bullet tore into his belly and he leaned against the car as he was knocked back a step. A last shot whipped his head around violently, and he dropped to the ground. Felipe started to put more bullets into the rifle but decided not to.

to unbuckle to undo the buckle

to whip to move abruptly

The two brothers walked to the car and stood over the still-moving body of Luis Baca. Antonio reached down and slid the police revolver out of the holster, took aim, and pulled the trigger.

trigger *Abzug*

"Luis Baca, the poor fool, made a feeble gurgle like a sick cat and went to hell.

"They will catch me, I know. There were people who saw us being chased by the cop. Antonio went to Albuquerque and he took the pistol. He will get caught too."

That was what he told me that night when we were sitting at the water tank. He used to tell me all kinds of things because I would listen. I liked those stories he told about the Korean war. That was where he learned how to drive a truck, and he had saved up his money so that he could buy a truck after he got out of the marines. Felipe and I used to go hunting and fishing too.

I sort of believed him, about the killing of Luis Baca the state cop, but not really, until a few days later when I heard my mother talking about it with my father. I asked something about it, and they told me to forget it and said that Felipe would probably die in the electric chair. Every night, for quite a while, I prayed a rosary or something for him.

rosary string of beads used by Catholics

Gay Talese, The Bridge

The story, published in 1964, tells an everyday episode of native Americans returning home from their work. Though the author concentrates on the short trip, he still manages to give the reader an idea of the living conditions, the work and the aspirations and dreams of these modern, so-called "Urban Indians".

Montour was a very handsome young man of twenty-six. He had blue eyes, sharp, very un-Indian facial features, almost blond hair. He was married to an extraordinary Indian beauty and had a two-year-old son, and each weekend Danny Montour drove up to the reservation to visit them. He had named his young son after his father, Mark, an ironworker who had crippled himself severely in an automobile accident and had died not long afterward. Danny's paternal grandfather had fallen with the Quebec Bridge in 1907, dying as a result of injuries. His maternal grandfather, also an ironworker, was drunk on the day of the Quebec disaster and, therefore, in no condition to climb the bridge. He later died in an automobile accident.

➊ What is so remarkable about the young Indian couple?

facial belonging to the face
features characteristics

Quebec disaster construction accident in which the partially-completed south arm of the Quebec bridge fell into the St Lawrence river on August 29th, 1907, killing 75 workmen.

Relate the description of the living conditions of modern Indians to the image you may have of the traditional Indian life.

Despite all this, Danny Montour, as a boy growing up, never doubted that he would become an ironworker. What else would bring such money and position on the reservation? To not become an ironworker was to become a farmer – and to be awakened at 2 A.M. by the automobile horns of returning ironworkers.

So, of the two thousand men on the reservation, few became farmers or clerks or gas pumpers, and fewer became doctors or lawyers, but 1,700 became ironworkers. They could not escape it. It got them when they were babies awakened in their cribs by the horns. The lights would go on, and their mothers would pick them up and bring them downstairs to their fathers, all smiling and full of money and smelling of whiskey or beer, and so happy to be home. They were incapable of enforcing discipline, only capable of handing dollar bills around for the children to play with, and all Indian children grew up with money in their hands. They liked the feel of it, later wanted more of it, *fast* – for fast cars, fast living, fast trips back and forth between long weekends and endless bridges.

to enforce to use authority or force to get sth done

"It's a good life," Danny Montour was trying to explain, driving his car up the Henry Hudson Parkway in New York, past the George Washington Bridge. "You can *see* the job, can see it shape up from a hole in the ground to a tall building or a big bridge."

He paused for a moment, then, looking through the side window at the New York skyline, he said, "You know, I have a name for this town. I don't know if anybody said it before, but I call this town the City of Man-made Mountains. And we're all part of it, and it gives you a good feeling – you're a kind of mountain builder ..."

Drinking alcohol is a serious problem which endangers the life of the Indian communities. Find examples to support this statement.

"That's right, Danny-boy, old kid," said Del Stacey, the Indian ironworker who was a little drunk, and sat in the front seat next to Montour with a half-case of beer and bag of ice under his feet. Stacey was a short, plump, copper-skinned young man wearing a straw hat with a red feather in it.

"Sometimes though," Montour continued, "I'd like to stay home more, and see more of my wife and kid ..."

"But we can't, Danny-boy," Stacey cut in, cheerfully. "We gotta build them mountains, Danny-boy, and let them women stay home alone, so they'll miss us and won't get a big head, right?" Stacey finished his bottle of beer, then opened a second one with his teeth. The third Indian, in the back seat, was quietly sleeping, having passed out.

They were not asked: The African-Americans

Harriet Jacobs, Scenes at the Plantation

This nineteenth-century autobiographical description by a female slave is remarkable in many ways. The chapters from *Incidents in the Life of a Slave Girl* show various aspects of life in slavery. This excerpt reveals not only the daily duties of a slave on a plantation but also her duties as a mother, a daughter and a sister as regards her own family which has been separated from her. On the other hand, it is an early document, not only of female emancipation, but even more of the awareness of the writer's role as a black member of society. It is also worth noting what it must have meant for an African-American girl in the middle of the nineteenth century to teach herself to read and write. The touch of sentimentality in her writing is probably attributable to the literary taste of her female readers at whom this variation of the then popular sentimental novel is primarily aimed. Last but not least, the well-balanced description tries to do justice to the issues of the slaves' misery and their yearning to be free while at the same time presenting a differentiated picture of the white masters and mistresses.

Early the next morning I left my grandmother's with my youngest child. My boy was ill, and I left him behind. I had many sad thoughts as the old wagon jolted on. Hitherto, I had suffered alone; now, my little one was to be treated as a slave. As we drew near the great house, I thought of the time when I was formerly sent there out of revenge. I wondered for what purpose I was now sent. I could not tell. I resolved to obey orders so far as duty required; but within myself, I determined to make my stay as short as possible. Mr. Flint was waiting to receive us, and told me to follow him upstairs to receive orders for the day. My little Ellen was left below in the kitchen. It was a change for her, who had always been so carefully tended. My young master said she might amuse herself in the yard. This was kind of him, since the child was hateful to his sight. My task was to fit up the house for the reception of the bride. In the midst of sheets, tablecloths, towels, drapery, and carpeting, my head was as busy planning, as were my fingers with the needle. At noon I was allowed to go to

Look for examples in the text of how slaves were treated by their white owners. What do they tell you about the character and motivation of the whites and about the political and social conditions in the South?

hitherto (old) up to this point

to tend to look after, take care of

to break in to teach how to obey rules, usually used of horses

a chip of the old block a child acting like its parents

Describe and interpret the differences in the attitudes of the different generations.

remonstrate (fml) to protest

lot here: a person's destiny, fortune or situation

Trace the description of the relationship between slave girl and master.

shingle flat stone for the roof

Ellen. She had sobbed herself to sleep. I heard Mr. Flint say to a neighbor, "I've got her down here, and I'll soon take the town notions out of her head. My father is partly to blame for her nonsense. He ought to have broke her in long ago." The remark was made within my hearing, and it would have been quite as manly to have made it to my face. He *had* said things to my face which might, or might not, have surprised his neighbor if he had known of them. He was "a chip of the old block."

I resolved to give him no cause to accuse me of being too much of a lady, so far as work was concerned. I worked day and night, with wretchedness before me. When I lay down beside my child, I felt how much easier it would be to see her die than to see her master beat her about, as I daily saw him beat other little ones. The spirit of the mothers was so crushed by the lash, that they stood by, without courage to remonstrate. How much more must I suffer, before I should be "broke in" to that degree?

I wished to appear as contented as possible. Sometimes I had an opportunity to send a few lines home; and this brought up recollections that made it difficult, for a time, to seem calm and indifferent to my lot. Notwithstanding my efforts, I saw that Mr. Flint regarded me with a suspicious eye. Ellen broke down under the trials of her new life. Separated from me, with no one to look after her, she wandered about, and in a few days cried herself sick. One day, she sat under the window where I was at work, crying that weary cry which makes a mother's heart bleed. I was obliged to steel myself to bear it. After a while it ceased. I looked out, and she was gone. As it was near noon, I ventured to go down in search of her. The great house was raised two feet above the ground. I looked under it, and saw her about midway, fast asleep. I crept under and drew her out. As I held her in my arms, I thought how well it would be for her if she never waked up; and I uttered my thought aloud. I was startled to hear some one say, "Did you speak to me?" I looked up, and saw Mr. Flint standing beside me. He said nothing further, but turned, frowning, away. That night he sent Ellen a biscuit and a cup of sweetened milk. This generosity surprised me. I learned afterwards, that in the afternoon he had killed a large snake, which crept from under the house; and I supposed that incident had prompted his unusual kindness.

The next morning the old cart was loaded with shingles for town. I put Ellen into it, and sent her to her grandmother. Mr. Flint said I ought to have asked his permission. I told him the child was sick, and required attention which I had no time to give. He let it pass; for he was aware that I had accomplished much work in a little time.

I had been three weeks on the plantation, when I planned a visit home. It must be at night, after every body was in bed. I was six miles from town, and the road was very dreary. I was to go with a young man, who, I knew, often stole to town to see his mother. One night, when all was quiet, we started. Fear gave speed to our steps, and we were not long in performing the journey. I arrived at my grandmother's. Her bed room was on the first floor, and the window was open, the weather being warm. I spoke to her and she awoke. She let me in and closed the window, lest some late passer-by should see me. A light was brought, and the whole household gathered round me, some smiling and some crying. I went to look at my children, and thanked God for their happy sleep. The tears fell as I leaned over them. As I moved to leave, Benny stirred. I turned back, and whispered, "Mother is here." After digging at his eyes with his little fist, they opened, and he sat up in bed, looking at me curiously. Having satisfied himself that it was I, he exclaimed, "O mother! you ain't dead, are you? They didn't cut off your head at the plantation, did they?"

My time was up too soon, and my guide was waiting for me. I laid Benny back in his bed, and dried his tears by a promise to come again soon. Rapidly we retraced our steps back to the plantation. About half way we were met by a company of four patrols. Luckily we heard their horse's hoofs before they came in sight, and we had time to hide behind a large tree. They passed, hallooing and shouting in a manner that indicated a recent carousal. How thankful we were that they had not their dogs with them! We hastened our footsteps, and when we arrived on the plantation we heard the sound of the hand-mill. The slaves were grinding their corn. We were safely in the house before the horn summoned them to their labor. I divided my little parcel of food with my guide, knowing that he had lost the chance of grinding his corn, and must toil all day in the field.

to summon to call

to toil to work

Mr. Flint often took an inspection of the house, to see that no one was idle. The entire management of the work was trusted to me, because he knew nothing about it; and rather than hire a superintendent he contented himself with my arrangements. He had often urged upon his father the necessity of having me at the plantation to take charge of his affairs, and make clothes for the slaves; but the old man knew him too well to consent to that arrangement.

When I had been working a month at the plantation, the great aunt of Mr. Flint came to make him a visit. This was the

➊ A different view of the whites.

good old lady who paid fifty dollars for my grandmother, for the purpose of making her free, when she stood on the auction block. My grandmother loved this old lady, whom we all called Miss Fanny. She often came to take tea with us. On such occasions the table was spread with a snow-white cloth, and the china cups and silver spoons were taken from the old-fashioned buffet. There were hot muffins, tea rusks, and delicious sweetmeats. My grandmother kept two cows, and the fresh cream was Miss Fanny's delight. She invariably declared that it was the best in town. The old ladies had cosey times together. They would work and chat, and sometimes, while talking over old times, their spectacles would get dim with tears, and would have to be taken off and wiped. When Miss Fanny bade us good by, her bag was filled with grandmother's best cakes, and she was urged to come again soon.

rusk *Zwieback*
sweetmeats (old) small, fancy cakes

Relate this description of ethnic and social relationships to the one above. ➔

There had been a time when Dr. Flint's wife came to take tea with us, and when her children were also sent to have a feast of "Aunt Marthy's" nice cooking. But after I became an object of her jealousy and spite, she was angry with grandmother for giving a shelter to me and my children. She would not even speak to her in the street. This wounded my grandmother's feelings, for she could not retain ill will against the woman whom she had nourished with her milk when a babe. The doctor's wife would gladly have prevented our intercourse with Miss Fanny if she could have done it, but fortunately she was not dependent on the bounty of the Flints. She had enough to be independent; and that is more than can ever be gained from charity, however lavish it may be.

to retain to keep, hold on to

intercourse here: communication

bounty a gift or reward, esp. money

Miss Fanny was endeared to me by many recollections, and I was rejoiced to see her at the plantation. The warmth of her large, loyal heart made the house seem pleasanter while she was in it. She staid a week, and I had many talks with her. She said her principal object in coming was to see how I was treated, and whether any thing could be done for me. She inquired whether she could help me in any way. I told her I believed not. She condoled with me in her own peculiar way; saying she wished that I and all my grandmother's family were at rest in our graves, for not until then should she feel any peace about us. The good old soul did not dream that I was planning to bestow peace upon her, with regard to myself and my children; not by death, but by securing our freedom.

to condole to express sympathy about sth painful or sad

to bestow upon to grant, to give

Again and again I had traversed those dreary twelve miles, to and from the town; and all the way, I was meditating upon some means of escape for myself and my children. My friends had made every effort that ingenuity could devise to effect our purchase, but all their plans had proved abortive. Dr. Flint was suspicious, and determined not to loosen his grasp upon us. I could have made my escape alone; but it was more for my helpless children than for myself that I longed for freedom. Though the boon would have been precious to me, above all price, I would not have taken it at the expense of leaving them in slavery. Every trial I endured, every sacrifice I made for their sakes, drew them closer to my heart, and gave me fresh courage to beat back the dark waves that rolled and rolled over me in a seemingly endless night of storms.

The six weeks were nearly completed, when Mr. Flint's bride was expected to take possession of her new home. The arrangements were all completed, and Mr. Flint said I had done well. He expected to leave home on Saturday, and return with his bride the following Wednesday. After receiving various orders from him, I ventured to ask permission to spend Sunday in town. It was granted; for which favor I was thankful. It was the first I had ever asked of him, and I intended it should be the last. It needed more than one night to accomplish the project I had in view; but the whole of Sunday would give me an opportunity. I spent the Sabbath with my grandmother. A calmer, more beautiful day never came down out of heaven. To me it was a day of conflicting emotions. Perhaps it was the last day I should ever spend under that dear, old sheltering roof! Perhaps these were the last talks I should ever have with the faithful old friend of my whole life! Perhaps it was the last time I and my children should be together! Well, better so, I thought, than that they should be slaves. I knew the doom that awaited my fair baby in slavery, and I determined to save her from it, or perish in the attempt.

ingenuity creative thinking in order to solve problems
purchase buying, being bought
abortive unsuccessful

boon (archaic) blessing, benefit

trial difficult situation

➊ Study the following description of a Sabbath and Sunday in detail.

to venture to dare to do

Harper Lee, To Kill a Mockingbird

The novel was first published in 1960, interestingly enough in Britain, as this was before the dramatic changes in self-awareness and public acceptance of the African-American minority in the US that were initiated by the Civil Rights Movement had begun to pick up momentum. The novel focuses on two themes that are closely linked with each other – the experiences of two children, Jem and Scout, who are growing up in the American South of the thirties and the trial of Tom Robinson, a black man unjustly accused of raping a white girl. The work of Harper Lee who was a young woman at the time, was made extremely popular through the film version, directed by Robert Mulligan, that appeared two years later. Gregory Peck played the role of Atticus Finch, the father of the two children and the lawyer selected to defend Tom Robinson. He takes up the fight despite negative public opinion and his sad insight that the defendant has not got a chance even though he, Atticus Finch, might be able to prove his innocence.

To get an idea of the historical background check any search engine for more information on the Internet under the keywords *John F. Kennedy, Martin Luther King, Rosa Parks.*

'You can just take that back, boy!'
This order, given by me to Cecil Jacobs, was the beginning of a rather thin time for Jem and me. My fists were clenched and I was ready to let fly. Atticus had promised me he would wear me out if he ever heard of me fighting any more; I was far too old and too big for such childish things, and the sooner I learned to hold in, the better off everybody would be. I soon forgot.
Cecil Jacobs made me forget. He had announced in the schoolyard the day before that Scout Finch's daddy defended niggers. I denied it, but told Jem.
'What'd he mean sayin' that?' I asked.
'Nothing,' Jem said. 'Ask Atticus, he'll tell you.'

The term used for African-Americans has changed over the years. Check the connotations of words like blacks, negroes, niggers, African-Americans.

'Do you defend niggers, Atticus?' I asked him that evening.
'Of course I do. Don't say nigger, Scout. That's common.'
''s what everybody at school says.'
'From now on it'll be everybody less one –'
'Well if you don't want me to grow up talkin' that way, why do you send me to school?'

dose portion

My father looked at me mildly, amusement in his eyes. Despite our compromise, my campaign to avoid school had continued in one form or another since my first day's dose of it: the beginning of last September had brought on sinking spells, dizziness, and mild gastric complaints. I went so far as to pay a nickel for the privilege of rubbing my head against the head of Miss Rachel's cook's son, who was afflicted with a tremendous ringworm. It didn't take.

to worry a bone to be strongly concerned with sth

But I was worrying another bone. 'Do all lawyers defend n-Negroes, Atticus?'
'Of course they do, Scout.'

still illegal distillery

'Then why did Cecil say you defended niggers? He made it sound like you were runnin' a still.'
Atticus sighed. 'I'm simply defending a Negro – his name's Tom Robinson. He lives in that little settlement beyond the town dump. He's a member of Calpurnia's church, and Cal knows his family well. She says they're clean-living folks.

Scout, you aren't old enough to understand some things yet, but there's been some high talk around town to the effect that I shouldn't do much about defending this man. It's a peculiar case – it won't come to trial until summer session. John Taylor was kind enough to give us a postponement ...'

John Taylor Judge's name
postponement extra time

'If you shouldn't be defendin' him, then why are you doin' it?'

'For a number of reasons,' said Atticus. 'The main one is, if I didn't I couldn't hold up my head in town, I couldn't represent this country in the legislature, I couldn't even tell you or Jem not to do something again.'

'You mean if you didn't defend that man, Jem and me wouldn't have to mind you any more?'

'That's about right.'

'Why?'

'Because I could never ask you to mind me again. Scout, simply by the nature of the work, every lawyer gets at least one case in his lifetime that affects him personally. This one's mine, I guess. You might hear some ugly talk about it at school, but do one thing for me if you will: you just hold your head high and keep those fists down. No matter what anybody says to you, don't you let 'em get your goat. Try fighting with your head for a change ... It's a good one, even if it does resist learning.'

to get sb's goat to bother or annoy

'Atticus, are we going to win it?'

'No, honey.'

'Then why –'

'Simply because we were licked a hundred years before we started is no reason for us not to try to win,' Atticus said.

to lick to strike repeatedly, to overcome

Waring Cuney, No Images

The poem is about different images: those that exist in the mind and the concrete ones. Analyse how the poet refers to a possible self-awareness.

She does not know
her beauty.
She thinks her brown body
has no glory.

➊ Awareness of her own beauty as a key to emancipation and equality: "Black is beautiful."

If she could dance
naked,
under palm trees
and see her image in the river
she would know.

But there are no palm trees
on the street,
and dish water gives back no image.

Langston Hughes, I, Too, Sing America

The poem can be seen as an answer to Walt Whitman's poem "I hear America singing". Within the frame of the first and the last verse, a development is sketched that will end in the full citizenship of the lyrical I, representative of all underprivileged African-Americans.

What do the two words in the term "darker brother" imply? What is the symbolic significance of the daily situations described?

I, too, sing America.

I am the darker brother.
They send me to eat in the kitchen
when company comes,
but I laugh
and eat well,
and grow strong.

Tomorrow
I'll sit at the table
when company comes.
Nobody'll dare
say to me,
"Eat in the kitchen"
then.

Besides,
they'll see how beautiful I am
and be ashamed –

I, too, am America.

From diaspora to diaspora: The Jewish Americans

Kurt Vonnegut, Jr., Adam

Birth and death are not only the most important moments in people's lives, they are great literary themes as well. The way in which people react to them says a lot about them and the culture they have grown up in and the values they cherish. Consider how the narrator uses this concept to throw light on the difference between Heinz and "the Americans."
Any educated reader has a certain image of Chicago which creates a particular scenery and lends a special atmosphere to the place. What is yours?
Think of what is in a name, a surname and a Christian name. What can they tell you about a national or regional context or family tradition?

It was midnight in a Chicago lying-in hospital.

"Mr. Sousa," said the nurse, "your wife had a girl. You can see the baby in about twenty minutes."

"I know, I know, I know," said Mr. Sousa, a sullen gorilla, plainly impatient with having a tiresome and familiar routine explained to him. He snapped his fingers. "Girl! Seven, now. Seven girls I got now. A houseful of women. I can beat the stuffings out of ten men my own size. But, what do I get? Girls."

"Mr. Knechtmann," said the nurse to the other man in the room. She pronounced the name, as almost all Americans did, a colorless Netman. "I'm sorry. Still no word on your wife. She is keeping us waiting, isn't she?" She grinned glassily and left.

Sousa turned on Knechtmann. "Some little son of a gun like you, Netman, you want a boy, bing! You got one. Want a football team, bing, bing, bing, eleven, you got it." He stomped out of the room.

The man he left behind, all alone now, was Heinz Knechtmann, a presser in a dry-cleaning plant, a small man with thin wrists and a bad spine that kept him slightly hunched, as though forever weary. His face was long and big-nosed and thin-lipped, but was so overcast with good-humored humility as to be beautiful. His eyes were large and brown, and deep-set and longlashed. He was only twenty-two, but seemed and felt much older. He had died a little as each member of his family

lying-in hospital where children are born

sullen silently bad-tempered

to beat the stuffings out of to win in a fight

son of a gun (ifml) guy

dry-cleaning plant *Reinigung*

spine backbone

hunched with bent shoulders

humility *Demut, Bescheidenheit*

had been led away and killed by the Nazis, until only in him, at the age of ten, had life and the name of Knechtmann shared a soul. He and his wife, Avchen, had grown up behind barbed wire.

barbed wire wire with short sharp points to stop prisoners escaping

He had been staring at the walls of the waiting room for twelve hours now, since noon, when his wife's labor pains had become regular, the surges of slow rollers coming in from the sea a mile apart, from far, far away. This would be his second child. The last time he had waited, he had waited on a straw tick in a displaced-persons camp in Germany. The child, Karl Knechtmann, named after Heinz's father, had died, and with it, once more, had died the name of one of the finest cellists ever to have lived.

labor pains *Wehen*

displaced person sb who cannot claim a home-country

When the numbness of weary wishing lifted momentarily during this second vigil, Heinz's mind was a medley of proud family names, gone, all gone, that could be brought to life again in this new being – if it lived. Peter Knechtmann, the surgeon; Kroll Knechtmann, the botanist; Friederich Knechtmann, the playwright. Dimly recalled uncles. Or if it was a girl, and if it lived, it would be Helga Knechtmann, Heinz's mother, and she would learn to play the harp as Heinz's mother had, and for all Heinz's ugliness, she would be beautiful. The Knechtmann men were all ugly, the Knechtmann women were all lovely as angels, though not all angels. It had always been so – for hundreds and hundreds of years.

medley confused or jumbled mixture

The significance of the "proud family names". ➊

"Mr. Netman," said the nurse, "it's a boy, and your wife is fine. She's resting now. You can see her in the morning. You can see the baby in twenty minutes."

Heinz looked up dumbly.

"It weighs five pounds nine ounces." She was gone again, with the same prim smile and officious, squeaking footsteps.

"Knechtmann," murmured Heinz, standing and bowing slightly to the wall. "The name is Knechtmann." He bowed again and gave a smile that was courtly and triumphant. He spoke the name with an exaggerated Old World pronunciation, like a foppish footman announcing the arrival of nobility, a guttural drum roll, unsoftened for American ears. *"KhhhhhhhhhhhhhhhNECHT! mannnnnnnnnnnnn."*

Both names, Knechtmann and Netman, can be interpreted as telling-names. What do they stand for? ➊

"Mr. Netman?" A very young doctor with a pink face and close-cropped red hair stood in the waiting-room door. There were circles under his eyes, and he spoke through a yawn.

"Dr. Powers!" cried Heinz, clasping the man's right hand between both of his. "Thank God, thank God, thank God, and thank you."

What do the reactions to the birth of the child reveal about the different characters? ➊

"Um," said Dr. Powers, and he managed to smile wanly.
"There isn't anything wrong, is there?"
"Wrong?" said Powers. "No, no. Everything's fine. If I look down in the mouth, it's because I've been up for thirty-six hours straight." He closed his eyes, and leaned against the doorframe. "No, no trouble with your wife," he said in a faraway voice. "She's made for having babies. Regular pop-up toaster. Like rolling off a log. Schnip-schnap."
"She is?" said Heinz incredulously.
Dr. Powers shook his head, bringing himself back to consciousness. "My mind – conked out completely. Sousa – I got your wife confused with Mrs. Sousa. They finished in a dead heat. Netman, you're Netman. Sorry. Your wife's the one with pelvis trouble."
"Malnutrition as a child," said Heinz.
"Yeah. Well, the baby came normally, but, if you're going to have another one, it'd better be a Caesarean. Just to be on the safe side."
"I can't thank you enough," said Heinz passionately.
Dr. Powers licked his lips, and fought to keep his eyes open. "Uh huh. 'S O.K.," he said thickly. "'Night. Luck." He shambled out into the corridor.
The nurse stuck her head into the waiting room. "You can see your baby, Mr. Netman."
"Doctor –" said Heinz, hurrying out into the corridor, wanting to shake Powers' hand again so that Powers would know what a magnificent thing he'd done. "It's the most wonderful thing that ever happened." The elevator doors slithered shut between them before Dr. Powers could show a glimmer of response.

"This way," said the nurse. "Turn left at the end of the hall, and you'll find the nursery window there. Write your name on a piece of paper and hold it against the glass."
Heinz made the trip by himself, without seeing another human being until he reached the end. There, on the other side of a large glass panel, he saw a hundred of them cupped in shallow canvas buckets and arranged in a square block of straight ranks and files.
Heinz wrote his name on the back of a laundry slip and pressed it to the window. A fat and placid nurse looked at the paper, not at Heinz's face, and missed seeing his wide smile, missed an urgent invitation to share for a moment his ecstasy.
She grasped one of the buckets and wheeled it before the window. She turned away again, once more missing the smile.

wan pale from stress or tiredness

to conk out to fail to work

pelvis *Becken*

malnutrition effect of scarce or bad food

Caesarean [sɪˈzeəriən] *Kaiserschnitt*

to slither to move smoothly

shallow not deep

laundry slip piece of paper to claim your laundry

placid not easily upset

prune dried plum

to beam here: to smile joyfully

cursory superficial

Could this little episode be left out? State what would be missed.

dank unpleasantly damp

"Hello, hello, hello, little Knechtmann," said Heinz to the red prune on the other side of the glass. His voice echoed down the hard, bare corridor, and came back to him with embarrassing loudness. He blushed and lowered his voice. "Little Peter, little Kroll," he said softly, "little Friederich – and there's Helga in you, too. Little spark of Knechtmann, you little treasure house. Everything is saved in you."

"I'm afraid you'll have to be more quiet," said a nurse, sticking her head out from one of the rooms.

"Sorry," said Heinz. "I'm very sorry." He fell silent, and contented himself with tapping lightly on the window with a fingernail, trying to get the child to look at him. Young Knechtmann would not look, wouldn't share the moment, and after a few minutes the nurse took him away again.

Heinz beamed as he rode on the elevator and as he crossed the hospital lobby, but no one gave him more than a cursory glance. He passed a row of telephone booths and there, in one of the booths with the door open, he saw a soldier with whom he'd shared the waiting room an hour before.

"Yeah, Ma – seven pounds six ounces. Got hair like Buffalo Bill. No, we we haven't had time to make up a name for her yet ... That you, Pa? Yup, mother and daughter doin' fine, just fine. Seven pounds six ounces. Nope, no name ... That you, Sis? Pretty late for you to be up, ain't it? Doesn't look like anybody yet. Let me talk to Ma again ... That you, Ma? Well, I guess that's all the news from Chicago. Now, Mom, Mom, take it easy – don't worry. It's a swell-looking baby, Mom. Just the hair looks like Buffalo Bill, and I said it as a joke, Mom. That's right, seven pounds six ounces ..."

There were five other booths, all empty, all open for calls to anyplace an earth. Heinz longed to hurry into one of them breathlessly, and tell the marvelous news. But there was no one to call, no one waiting for the news.

But Heinz still beamed, and he strode across the street and into a quiet tavern there. In the dank twilight there were only two men, tête-à-tête, the bartender and Mr. Sousa.

"Yes sir, what'll it be?"

"I'd like to buy you and Mr. Sousa a drink," said Heinz with a heartiness strange to him. "I'd like the best brandy you've got. My wife just had a baby!"

"That so?" said the bartender with polite interest.

"Five pounds nine ounces," said Heinz.

"Huh," said the bartender. "What do you know."

"Netman," said Sousa, "wha'dja get?"

"Boy," said Heinz proudly.

"Never knew it to fail," said Sousa bitterly. "It's the little guys, all the time the little guys."

"Boy, girl," said Heinz, "it's all the same, just as long as it lives. Over there in the hospital, they're too close to it to see the wonder of it. A miracle over and over again – the world made new."

"Wait'll you've racked up seven, Netman," said Sousa. *"Then* you come back and tell me about the miracle."

to rack up to achieve, to score

"You got seven?" said the bartender. "I'm one up on you. I got eight." He poured three drinks.

"Far as I'm concerned," said Sousa, "you can have the championship."

Heinz lifted his glass. "Here's long life and great skill and much happiness to – to Peter Karl Knechtmann." He breathed quickly, excited by the decision.

Study how the reference to the child's first name is varied in the dialogue.

"There's a handle to take ahold of," said Sousa. "You'd think the kid weighed two hundred pounds."

"Peter is the name of a famous surgeon," said Heinz, "the boy's great-uncle, dead now. Karl was my father's name."

"Here's to Pete K. Netman," said Sousa, with a cursory salute.

"Pete," said the bartender, drinking.

"And here's to *your* little girl – the new one," said Heinz.

Sousa sighed and smiled wearily. "Here's to her. God bless her."

"And now, *I'll* propose a toast," said the bartender, hammering on the bar with his fist. "On your feet, gentlemen. Up, up, everybody up."

Heinz stood, and held his glass high, ready for the next step in camaraderie, a toast to the whole human race, of which the Knechtmanns were still a part.

"Here's to the White Sox!" roared the bartender.

"Minoso, Fox, Mele," said Sousa.

"Fain, Lollar, Rivera!" said the bartender. He turned to Heinz. "Drink up, boy! The White Sox! Don't tell me you're a Cub fan."

"No," said Heinz, disappointed. "No – I don't follow baseball, I'm afraid." The other two men seemed to be sinking away from him. "I haven't been able to think about much but the baby."

The bartender at once turned his full attention to Sousa. "Look," he said intensely, "they take Fain off of first, and put him at third, and give Pierce first. Then move Minoso in from left field to shortstop. See what I'm doing?"

"Yep, yep," said Sousa eagerly.

"And then we take that no-good Carrasquel and ..."

Heinz was all alone again, with twenty feet of bar between him and the other two men. It might as well have been a continent.

He finished his drink without pleasure, and left quietly.

At the railroad station, where he waited for a local train to take him home to the South Side, Heinz's glow returned again as he saw a co-worker at the dry-cleaning plant walk in with a girl. They were laughing and had their arms around each other's waist.

"Harry," said Heinz, hurrying toward them. "Guess what, Harry. Guess what just happened." He grinned broadly.

dapper neat and smart in appearance
snub-nosed short, flat nose with the tip turned up

Harry, a tall, dapper, snub-nosed young man, looked down at Heinz with mild surprise. "Oh – hello, Heinz. What's up, boy?"

to accost to address, to speak to
derisive [dɪˈraɪsɪv] scornful, mocking

The girl looked on in perplexity, as though asking why they should be accosted at such an odd hour by such an odd person. Heinz avoided her slightly derisive eyes.

"A baby, Harry. My wife just had a boy."

limp lacking strength

"Oh," said Harry. He extended his hand. "Well, congratulations." The hand was limp. "I think that's swell, Heinz, perfectly swell." He withdrew his hand and waited for Heinz to say something else.

"Yes, yes – just about an hour ago," said Heinz. "Five pounds nine ounces. I've never been happier in my life."

"Well, I think it's perfectly swell, Heinz. You should be happy."

"Yes, indeed," said the girl.

There was a long silence, with all three shifting from one foot to the other.

"Really good news," said Harry at last.

"Yes, well," said Heinz quickly, "well, that's all I had to tell you."

"Thanks," said Harry. "Glad to hear about it."

There was another uneasy silence.

jaunty carefree, self-confident

"See you at work," said Heinz, and strode jauntily back to his bench, but with his reddened neck betraying how foolish he felt.

The girl giggled.

bassinet *Korbwiege, Kinderwagen*

How is Heinz's reflection supported by history and personal experience?

Back home in his small apartment, at two in the morning, Heinz talked to himself, to the empty bassinet, and to the bed. He talked in German, a language he had sworn never to use again.

to shrug to raise one's shoulders to express indifference

"They don't care," said Heinz. "They're all too busy, busy, busy to notice life, to feel anything about it. A baby is born." He shrugged. "What could be duller? Who would be so stupid as to talk about it, to think there was anything important or interesting about it?"

He opened a window on the summer night, and looked out at the moonlit canyon of gray wooden porches and garbage cans.

"There are too many of us, and we are all too far apart," said Heinz. "Another Knechtmann is born, another O'Leary, another Sousa. Who cares? Why should anyone care? What difference does it make? None."

He lay down in his clothes on the unmade bed, and, with a rattling sigh, went to sleep.

He awoke at six, as always. He drank a cup of coffee, and with a wry sense of anonymity, he jostled and was jostled aboard the downtown train. His face showed no emotion. It was like all the other faces, seemingly incapable of surprise or wonder, joy or anger.

He walked across town to the hospital with the same detachment, a gray, uninteresting man, a part of the city.

In the hospital, he was as purposeful and calm as the doctors and nurses bustling about him. When he was led into the ward where Avchen slept behind white screens, he felt only what he had always felt in her presence – love and aching awe and gratitude for her.

"You go ahead and wake her gently, Mr. Netman," said the nurse.

"Avchen –" He touched her on her white-gowned shoulder. "Avchen. Are you all right, Avchen?"

"Mmmmmmmmmm?" murmured Avchen. Her eyes opened to narrow slits. "Heinz. Hello, Heinz."

"Sweetheart, are you all right?"

"Yes, yes," she whispered. "I'm fine. How is the baby, Heinz?"

"Perfect. Perfect, Avchen."

"They couldn't kill us, could they, Heinz?"

"No."

"And here we are, alive as we can be."

"The baby, Heinz –" She opened her dark eyes wide. "It's the most wonderful thing that ever happened, isn't it?"

"Yes," said Heinz.

wry embittered, ironical
to jostle to push roughly

detachment lack of interest

to bustle to move about quickly
ward division of a hospital, *Station*
to ache to have a continuous pain
awe *Ehrfurcht*

What does the dialogue between Heinz and Avchen illustrate? Check the etymology of the name Eve/Ava.

Swept across from different shores: The Asian-Americans

Lan Cao, Monkey Bridge

The novel with its telling title of *Monkey Bridge,* a fragile bridge built of bamboo and used in Vietnam for centuries, tells a story which tries to bridge two worlds. One is the world of the daughter who has outgrown the first years of Vietnamese immigrant experience in the United States, the other one is that of her mother who is deeply rooted in her past in Vietnam and alienated from a culture she finds difficult to cope with. Her daughter not only has to play the role of translator and mediator between the East and the West, but also between the past and the present.

Khe Sanh Vietnam battlefield
Tet Offensive regarded as the turning point of the Vietnam war
Ho Chi Minh Trail named after the North Vietnamese leader

Various forms of misunderstanding, ambiguity, deception and illusion characterise the immigrant's world. Look for examples and sketch their significance.

unadulterated not spoiled, not morally corrupted
adult, adultery, adulterer, adulteress

to decipher to decode

temptation strong desire to do sth that is wrong or forbidden
to tempt

By the time I left Farmington to be with my mother, I had already created for myself a different, more sacred tongue. Khe Sanh, the Tet Offensive, the Ho Chi Minh Trail – a history as imperfect as my once obviously imperfect English – these were things that had rushed me into the American melting pot. And when I saw my mother again, I was no longer the same person she used to know. Inside my new tongue, my real tongue, was an astonishing new power. For my mother and her Vietnamese neighbors, I became the keeper of the word, the only one with access to the lightworld. Like Adam, I had the God-given right to name all the fowls of the air and all the beasts of the field.

The right to name, I quickly discovered, also meant the right to stand guard over language and the right to claim unadulterated authority. Here was a language with an ocean's quiet mystery, and it would be up to me to render its vastness comprehensible to the newcomers around me. My language skill, my ability to decipher the nuances of American life, was what held us firmly in place, night after night, in our Falls Church living room. The ease with which I could fabricate wholly new plot lines from TV made the temptation to invent especially difficult to resist.

And since my mother couldn't understand half of what anyone was saying, television watching, for me, was translating and more. This, roughly, was how things went in our living room:

The Bionic Woman had just finished rescuing a young girl, approximately my age, from drowning in a lake where she'd gone swimming against her mother's wishes. Once out of harm's way, Jaime made the girl promise she'd be more careful next time and listen to her mother.

Translation: the Bionic Woman rescued the girl from drowning in the lake, but commended her for her magnificent deeds, since the girl had heroically jumped into the water to rescue a prized police dog.

"Where's the dog?" my mother would ask. "I don't see him."

"He's not there anymore, they took him to the vet right away. Remember?" I sighed deeply.

"Oh," my mother said. "It's strange. Strong girl, Bionic Woman."

The dog that I convinced her existed on the television screen was no more confusing than the many small reversals in logic and the new identities we experienced her first few months in America.

"I can take you in this aisle," a store clerk offered as she unlocked a new register to accommodate the long line of customers. She gestured us to "come over here" with an upturned index finger, a disdainful hook we Vietnamese use to summon dogs and other domestic creatures. My mother did not understand the ambiguity of American hand gestures. In Vietnam, we said "Come here" to humans differently, with our palm up and all four fingers waved in unison – the way people over here waved goodbye. A typical Vietnamese signal beckoning someone to "come here" would prompt, in the United States, a "goodbye," a response completely opposite from the one desired.

"Even the store clerks look down on us," my mother grumbled as we walked home. This was a truth I was only beginning to realize: it was not the enormous or momentous event, but the gradual suggestion of irrevocable and protracted change that threw us off balance and made us know in no uncertain terms that we would not be returning to the familiarity of our former lives.

It was, in many ways, a lesson in what was required to sustain a new identity: it all had to do with being able to adopt a different posture, to reach deep enough into the folds of the earth to relocate one's roots and bend one's body in a new direction, pretending at the same time that the world was the same now as it had been the day before. I strove for the ability to realign my eyes, to shift with a shifting world and convince both myself and the rest of the world into thinking

Bionic Woman female TV heroine

to commend to praise

vet (ifml) short for veterinary surgeon

aisle here: *Gang, Reihe*

➊ The difference of sign language.

ambiguity double meaning

irrevocable final, definite

protracted over a long period of time

➊ Outline the lesson in "new identity".

to strive to work hard

to realign to adjust back into focus

endeavo(u)r serious effort

compulsion irresistible desire to do sth
compulsive, to compel

to deceive to trick and lie
deception, deceptive, deceit, deceitful

Explain the contrast between identification and identity.

to make up here: to form part of

refugee sb who flees for safety

to heave to lift or throw with great effort

Vietcong North Vietnam (Communist) army and underground fighters
draft dodger *Wehrdienst-verweigerer*

spin here: interpretation

that, if the earth moved and I moved along with it, that motion, however agitated, would be undetectable. The process, which was as surprising as a river reversing course and flowing upstream, was easier said than done.

All of Little Saigon maneuvered to pull the experiment off. The obsession with optical illusion was something I might have learned from my mother's friends. It became something of a community endeavor, the compulsion to deceive. Mrs. Bay, whose name translated literally into "Mrs. Seven," since she was the seventh child in her family, gave herself a new birthday the day she applied for her Social Security card, for no other reason than that she no longer wanted to be associated with the Year of the Rat. Her husband, who had died years before, had been born in the Year of the Cat. Spurred by the ease with which all of us could produce new identities, Mrs. Bay made herself two years younger and became, in one easy revolutionary twist, a tiger toying with a domesticated pet. "When I see him again in the next life, I will be the boss," she said, laughing. "That crazy old cat will expect to see a rat, but he'll see a tiger instead." In their new shadow warfare, Mrs. Bay would resurrect old battles she had once fought against her husband and rewrite the endings.

Like all of us who made up the refugee community, Little Saigon too was preoccupied with the possibility of astrological and historical revisions. It was as if the refugee portion of Falls Church decided that it would simply stretch its limbs, lean into the wind, and heave itself in a new, untried direction. Little Saigon was the still-tender, broken-off part of the old, old world, and over here, so far away from the old country, our ghosts could roam unattached to the old personalities we once inhabited. There was an odd element of righteousness in this transformation. Out of the ruins came a clatter of new personalities. A bar girl who once worked at Saigon's Queen Bee, a nightclub frequented by American soldiers, acquired a past as a virtuous Confucian teacher from a small village in a distant province. Here, in the vehemently anti-Vietcong refugee community, draft dodgers and ordinary foot soldiers could become decorated veterans of battlefields as famous as Kontum and Pleiku and Xuan Loc. It was the Vietnamese version of the American Dream; a new spin, the Vietnam spin, to the old immigrant faith in the future. Not only could we become anything we wanted to be in America, we could change what we had once been in Vietnam. Rebirthing the past, we called it, claiming what had once been a power reserved only for gods and other immortal beings.

The absence of documentation was not surprising. Even those with identification papers burned them before any authority could see. There was, after all, something awesome about a truly uncluttered beginning, the complete absence of identity, of history.

awesome inspiring awe *(Ehrfurcht)*

Amy Tan, Harold and I

In her novel *The Joy Luck Club,* an assembly of episodes is told by a first-person narrator, a Chinese-American woman. She takes on different roles and reflects on various situations and walks of life, which all have in common that they are rooted in the confrontation of two fundamentally different cultures and ways of life. The episodes illustrate how difficult the theoretical concept of integration can be when it comes to the reality of living and working together. This is particularly clear in the following episode which deals with the difficulties of both an inter-cultural business partnership and, more importantly the inter-cultural marriage of a Chinese woman and an American man.
As regards the nature and the consequences of the inter-cultural conflict, a comparison with Anchee Min is strongly recommended.

Harold and I work at the same architectural firm, Livotny & Associates. Only Harold Livotny is a partner and I am an associate. We met eight years ago, before he started Livotny & Associates. I was twenty-eight, a project assistant, and he was thirty-four. We both worked in the restaurant design and development division of Harned Kelley & Davis.
We started seeing each other for working lunches, to talk about the projects, and we would always split the tab right in half, even though I usually ordered only a salad because I have this tendency to gain weight easily. Later, when we started meeting secretly for dinner, we still divided the bill.
And we just continued that way, everything right down the middle. If anything, I encouraged it. Sometimes I insisted on paying for the whole thing: meal, drinks, and tip. And it really didn't bother me.
"Lena, you're really extraordinary," Harold said after six months of dinners, five months of post-prandial love-making, and one week of timid and silly love confessions. We were lying in bed, between new purple sheets I had just bought for

Examine the conditions of that business partnership.

tab bill

prandial of or relating to a meal

timid fearful or shy

him. His old set of white sheets was stained in revealing places, not very romantic.

to nuzzle to rub against gently

And he nuzzled my neck and whispered, "I don't think I've ever met another woman, who's so together ..." – and I remember feeling a hiccup of fear upon hearing the words "another woman," because I could imagine dozens, hundreds of adoring women eager to buy Harold breakfast, lunch, and dinner to feel the pleasure of his breath on their skin.

squishy here: soft and slightly fat
to swoon to be dizzy with joy

Then he bit my neck and said in a rush, "Nor anyone who's as soft and squishy and lovable as you are."

And with that, I swooned inside, caught off balance by this latest revelation of love, wondering how such a remarkable person as Harold could think I was extraordinary.

Comment on "that feeling of fear" in "women like us".

to dredge up to dig or pull out

Now that I'm angry at Harold, it's hard to remember what was so remarkable about him. And I know they're there, the good qualities, because I wasn't that stupid to fall in love with him, to marry him. All I can remember is how awfully lucky I felt, and consequently how worried I was that all this undeserved good fortune would someday slip away. When I fantasized about moving in with him, I also dredged up my deepest fears: that he would tell me I smelled bad, that I had terrible bathroom habits, that my taste in music and television was appalling. I worried that Harold would someday get a new prescription for his glasses and he'd put them on one morning, look me up and down, and say, "Why, gosh, you aren't the girl I thought you were, are you?"

sham (ifml) fake

And I think that feeling of fear never left me, that I would be caught someday, exposed as a sham of a woman. But recently, a friend of mine, Rose, who's in therapy now because her marriage has already fallen apart, told me those kinds of thoughts are commonplace in women like us.

humility *Demut, Unterwürfigkeit*

Tao teaching of Lao Tse, Chinese philosopher, 600 BC

baby boomers the post-war generation

diminishing returns effort put in does not produce the results wanted

"At first I thought it was because I was raised with all this Chinese humility," Rose said. "Or that maybe it was because when you're Chinese you're supposed to accept everything, flow with the Tao and not make waves. But my therapist said, Why do you blame your culture, your ethnicity? And I remembered reading an article about baby boomers, how we expect the best and when we get it we worry that maybe we should have expected more, because it's all diminishing returns after a certain age."

Explain Lena's efforts to deal with her fears rationally.

raving producing admiration

And after my talk with Rose, I felt better about myself and I thought, Of course, Harold and I are equals, in many respects. He's not exactly handsome in the classic sense, although clear-skinned and certainly attractive in that wiry intellectual way. And I may not be a raving beauty, but a lot of women in my aerobics class tell me I'm "exotic" in an unusual way, and they're jealous that my breasts don't sag, now that small breasts are in. Plus, one of my clients said I have incredible vitality and exuberance.

exuberance extreme joy

So I think I deserve someone like Harold, and I mean in the good sense and not like bad karma. We're equals. I'm also smart. I have common sense. And I'm intuitive, highly so. I was the one who told Harold he was good enough to start his own firm.

karma work that in Hinduist and Buddhist belief enables a person to transmigrate to a higher spiritual level

When we were still working at Harned Kelley & Davis, I said, "Harold, this firm knows just what a good deal it has with you. You're the goose who lays the golden egg. If you started your own business today, you'd walk away with more than half of the restaurant clients."

And he said, laughing, "Half? Boy, that's love."

And I shouted back, laughing with him, "More than half! You're that good. You're the best there is in restaurant design and development. You know it and I know it, and so do a lot of restaurant developers."

That was the night he decided to "go for it," as he put it, which is a phrase I have personally detested ever since a bank I used to work for adopted the slogan for its employee productivity contest.

employee sb who works for sb else
contest competition

But still, I said to Harold, "Harold, I want to help you go for it, too. I mean, you're going to need money to start this business."

He wouldn't hear of taking any money from me, not as a favor, not as a loan, not as an investment, or even as the down payment on a partnership. He said he valued our relationship too much. He didn't want to contaminate it with money. He explained, "I wouldn't want a handout any more than you'd want one. As long as we keep the money thing separate, we'll always be sure of our love for each other."

➊ Analyse Harold's arguments and behaviour closely.

to contaminate to pollute

I wanted to protest. I wanted to say, "No! I'm not really this way about money, the way we've been doing it. I'm really into giving freely. I want ..." But I didn't know where to begin. I wanted to ask him who, what woman, had hurt him this way, that made him so scared about accepting love in all its wonderful forms. But then I heard him saying what I'd been waiting to hear for a long, long time.

"Actually, you could help me out if you moved in with me. I mean, that way I could use the five hundred dollars' rent you paid to me ..."

"That's a wonderful idea," I said immediately, knowing how embarrassed he was to have to ask me that way. I was so deliriously happy that it didn't matter that the rent on my

delirious excited beyond control

studio was really only four hundred thirty-five. Besides, Harold's place was much nicer, a two-bedroom flat with a two-hundred-forty-degree view of the bay. It was worth the extra money, no matter whom I shared the place with.

So within the year, Harold and I quit Harned Kelley & Davis and he started Livotny & Associates, and I went to work there as a project coordinator. And no, he didn't get half the restaurant clients of Harned Kelley & Davis. In fact, Harned Kelley & Davis threatened to sue if he walked away with even one client over the next year. So I gave him pep talks in the evening when he was discouraged. I told him how he should do more avant-garde thematic restaurant design, to differentiate himself from the other firms.

pep talk short speech intended to encourage sb to work harder

"Who needs another brass and oakwood bar and grill?" I said. "Who wants another pasta place in sleek Italian moderno? How many places can you go to with police cars lurching out of the walls? This town is chockablock with restaurants that are just clones of the same old themes. You can find a niche. Do something different every time. Get the Hong Kong investors who are willing to sink some bucks into American ingenuity."

chockablock crowded

He gave me his adoring smile, the one that said, "I love it when you're so naive." And I adored his looking at me like that.

So I stammered out my love. "You ... you ... could do new theme eating places ... a ... a ... Home on the Range! All the home-cooked mom stuff, mom at the kitchen range with a gingham apron and mom waitresses leaning over telling you to finish your soup.

gingham plain cotton cloth, esp. striped or checked

"And maybe ... maybe you could do a novel-menu restaurant ... foods from fiction ... sandwiches from Lawrence Sanders murder mysteries, just desserts from Nora Ephron's *Heartburn*. And something else with a magic theme, or jokes and gags, or ..."

Harald actually listened to me. He took those ideas and he applied them in an educated, methodical way. He made it happen. But still, I remember, it was my idea.

And today Livotny & Associates is a growing firm of twelve full-time people, which specializes in thematic restaurant design, what I still like to call "theme eating." Harold is the concept man, the chief architect, the designer, the person who makes the final sales presentation to a new client. I work under the interior designer, because, as Harold explains, it would not seem fair to the other employees if he promoted me just because we are now married – that was five years ago, two years after he started Livotny & Associates. And even though I am very good at what I do, I have never been formally trained in this area. When I was majoring in Asian-American studies, I took only one relevant course, in theater set design, for a college production of *Madama Butterfly*. At Livotny & Associates, I procure the theme elements. For one restaurant called The Fisherman's Tale, one of my prized findings was a yellow varnished wood boat stenciled with the name "Overbored," and I was the one who thought the menus should dangle from miniature fishing poles, and the napkins be printed with rulers that have inches translating into feet. For a Lawrence of Arabia deli called Tray Sheik, I was the one who thought the place should have a bazaar effect, and I found the replicas of cobras lying on fake Hollywood boulders.

to major main subject of a student at university

Madama Butterfly opera by Giacomo Puccini about the love of a Japanese lady

to procure to obtain

boulder *Felsbrocken*

I love my work when I don't think about it too much. And when I do think about it, how much I get paid, how hard I work, how fair Harold is to everybody except me, I get upset. So really, we're equals, except that Harold makes about seven times more than what I make. He knows this, too, because he signs my monthly check, and then I deposit it into my separate checking account.

Explain the use of the term "equal" in this context.

Lately, however, this business about being equals started to bother me. It's been on my mind, only I didn't really know it. I just felt a little uneasy about *something*. And then about a week ago, it all became clear. I was putting the breakfast dishes away and Harold was warming up the car so we could go to work. And I saw the newspaper spread open on the kitchen counter, Harold's glasses on top, his favorite coffee mug with the chipped handle off to the side. And for some reason, seeing all these little domestic signs of familiarity, our daily ritual, made me swoon inside. But it was as if I were seeing Harold the first time we made love, this feeling of surrendering everything to him, with abandon, without caring what I got in return.

chipped having a small piece broken off

And when I got into the car, I still had the glow of that feeling and I touched his hand and said, "Harold, I love you." And he looked in the rearview mirror, backing up the car, and said, "I love you, too. Did you lock the door?" And just like that, I started to think, It's just not enough.

David Guterson, Snow Falling on Cedars

This courtroom-based novel (cf. Harper Lee, p. 47) reports on the trial of a Japanese-American fisherman accused of murder. As the circumstances of the case are unravelled, the reader is introduced to the life of the Japanese-American population in the North-West of the United States after the Japanese attack on Pearl Harbour in 1941. The ethnic and political conflict is reflected and intensified in the love between the young Japanese-born Hatsue and her friend Ishmael, a "white" American. The decision to give up her love for Ishmael is also a decision to embrace her ethnic identity.

Hatsue's mother gathered her five daughters together, Hisao's letters in her hand. She told her daughters, once again, the story of her odyssey from Japan on board the *Korea Maru*. She told them about the Seattle rooms she had cleaned, the sheets on which white men had vomited blood, the toilets full of their excrement, the stench of their alcohol and sweat. She told them about the waterfront cookhouse where she'd worked chopping onions and frying potatoes for *hakujin* stevedores who looked right through her as if she weren't even there. She knew, already, about hardship, she said – her life had long been difficult. She knew what it was to be alive without being alive; she knew what it was to be invisible. She wanted her daughters to know how to face this in a manner that would allow them their dignity. Hatsue sat motionless while her mother spoke, trying to guess at her meaning. She was eighteen now, and her mother's story held more weight than it had when she'd heard it earlier. She leaned forward and listened carefully. Her mother predicted that the war with Japan would force all her daughters to decide who they were and then to become more Japanese. Wasn't it true that the *hakujin* didn't really want them in their country? There were rumors that all the Japanese on the coast were going to be forced to leave. There was no point in trying to conceal anything or in trying to pretend they were not Japanese – the *hakujin* could see it in their faces; they were going to have to accept this. They were Japanese girls in America during a time when America was fighting a war with Japan – did any of them want to deny it? The trick was to live here without hating yourself because all around you was hatred. The trick was to refuse to allow your pain to prevent you from living honorably. In Japan, she said, a person learned not to complain or be distracted by suffering. To persevere was always a reflection of the state of one's inner life, one's philosophy, and one's

The author uses literary associations. What is the implication of his reference to the *Odyssey?*

stench very bad smell

hakujin Japanese for Americans

stevedore sb who loads and unloads ships

to hold more weight to be more significant

Fujiko switches between Japanese and English but always speaks of the *hakujin* instead of the Americans. Explain.

rumor hearsay, gossip

to conceal to hide

to persevere to carry on even when things are difficult

perspective. It was best to accept old age, death, injustice, hardship – all of these were part of living. Only a foolish girl would deny this was so, thus revealing to the world her immaturity and the degree to which she lived in the world of the *hakujin* instead of in the world of her own people. And her people, insisted Fujiko, were Japanese – the events of the past months had proved it so; why else had their father been arrested? The events of the last two months should teach them something about the darkness in the hearts of the *hakujin* and the more general darkness that was part of living. To deny that there was this dark side to life would be like pretending that the cold of winter was somehow only a temporary illusion, a way station on the way to the higher "reality" of long, warm, pleasant summers. But summer, it turned out, was no more real than the snow that melted in wintertime. Well, said Fujiko, now your father is gone, folding laundry in a camp in Montana, and we all must get by, endure. "Do you understand?" she said in Japanese. "There is no choice in the matter. We will all have to endure."

immaturity state of not being fully developed

Interpret the prevailing use of the colour metaphor.

"They don't all hate us," Hatsue replied. "You're exaggerating, mother – you know you are. They're not so different from us, you know. Some hate, others don't. It isn't all of them."

"I know what you're saying," said Fujiko. "Not all of them hate – you're correct. But on this other matter" – she still spoke in Japanese – "you don't think they are very much different? In some big way, Hatsue? Different from us?"

"No," said Hatsue. "I don't."

"They are," said Fujiko, "and I can tell you how. The whites, you see, are tempted by their egos and have no means to resist. We Japanese, on the other hand, *know* our egos are nothing. We bend our egos, all of the time, and that is where we differ. That is the fundamental difference, Hatsue. We bend our heads, we bow and are silent, because we understand that by ourselves, alone, we are nothing at all, dust in a strong wind, while the *hakujin* believes his aloneness is everything, his separateness is the foundation of his existence. He seeks and grasps, seeks and grasps for his separateness, while we seek union with the Greater Life – you must see that these are distinct paths we are travelling. Hatsue, the *hakujin* and we Japanese."

To what extent is Fujiko's description of the American way of life influenced by her Japanese philosophy? Find more examples.

"These people seeking union with the Greater Life," argued Hatsue, "are the ones who bombed Pearl Harbor. If they're so ready to bend and bow, then what are they doing attacking all over the world and taking over other countries? I don't feel I'm a part of them," said Hatsue. "I'm a part of *here*," she added. "I'm from this place."

"Yes, you were born here, that's so," said Fujiko. "But your blood – you are still Japanese."

"I don't want to be!" said Hatsue. "I don't want anything to do with them! Do you hear me? I don't want to be Japanese!"

What is Fujiko referring to? Check the historical context.

Fujiko nodded at her eldest daughter. "These are difficult times," she replied. "Nobody knows who they are now. Everything is cloudy and unclear. Still, you should learn to say nothing that will cause you regret. You should not say what is not in your heart – or what is only in your heart for a moment. But you know this – silence is better."

serene calm
unruffled not worried

to unravel to separate
thread *Faden, Geflecht*

Hatsue knew immediately that her mother was right. Her mother, clearly, was serene and unruffled, and her voice carried the strength of truth. Hatsue fell silent, ashamed of herself. Who was she to say how she felt? What she felt remained a mystery, she felt a thousand things at once, she could not unravel the thread of her feelings with enough certainty to speak with any accuracy. Her mother was right, silence was better. It was something – one thing – she knew with clarity.

What do the images Fujiko uses to describe the Americans have in common?

to decay to fall into ruin

"I could say," her mother went on, "that living among the *hakujin* has tainted you, made your soul impure, Hatsue. This lack of purity envelops you – I see it every day. You carry it with you always. It is like a mist around your soul, and it haunts your face like a shadow at moments when you do not protect it well. I see it in your eagerness to leave here and walk in the woods in the afternoon. I cannot translate all of this easily, except as the impurity that comes with living each day among the white people. I am not asking you to shun them entirely – this you should not do. You must live in this world, of course you must, and this world is the world of the *hakujin* – you must learn to live in it, you must go to school. But don't allow living *among* the *hakujin* to become living *intertwined* with them. Your soul will decay. Something fundamental will rot and go sour. You are eighteen, you are grown now – I can't walk with you where you are going anymore. You walk alone soon, Hatsue. I hope you will carry your purity with you always and remember the truth of who you are."

Just south of the border: The Mexican-Americans

Sandra Cisneros, No Speak English

Sandra Cisneros' story covers the many facets of immigration ranging from total rejection of the new country to gradual stages of pragmatic assimilation. The traditional roles of men and women and the mastery of language play an important role.

Mamacita is the big mama of the man across the street, third-floor front. Rachel says her name ought to be *Mamasota,* but I think that's mean.

mamacita (Span.) little mum
mamasota (Span.) big mum

The man saved his money to bring her here. He saved and saved because she was alone with the baby boy in that country. He worked two jobs. He came home late and he left early. Every day.

➊ Show to what extent the narrator steers the reader's first impressions through the description of husband and wife, and in particular, the use of irony.

Then one day *Mamacita* and the baby boy arrived in a yellow taxi. The taxi door opened like a waiter's arm. Out stepped a tiny pink shoe, a foot soft as a rabbit's ear, then the thick ankle, a flutter of hips, fuchsia roses and green perfume. The man had to pull her, the taxicab driver had to push. Push, pull. Push, pull. Poof!

All at once she bloomed. Huge, enormous, beautiful to look at, from the salmon-pink feather on the tip of her hat down to the little rosebuds of her toes. I couldn't take my eyes off her tiny shoes.

Up, up, up the stairs she went with the baby boy in a blue blanket, the man carrying her suitcases, her lavender hatboxes, a dozen boxes of satin high heels. Then we didn't see her.

Somebody said because she's too fat, somebody because of the three flights of stairs, but I believe she doesn't come out because she is afraid to speak English, and maybe this is so since she only knows eight words. She knows to say: *He not here* for when the landlord comes, *No speak English* if anybody else comes, and *Holy smokes*. I don't know where she learned this, but I heard her say it one time and it surprised me.

landlord house-owner letting his property for rent

My father says when he came to this country he ate hamandeggs for three months. Breakfast, lunch and dinner. Hamandeggs. That was the only word he knew. He doesn't eat hamandeggs anymore.

Whatever her reasons, whether she is fat, or can't climb the stairs, or is afraid of English, she won't come down. She sits all day by the window and plays the Spanish radio show and sings all the homesick songs about her country in a voice that sounds like a seagull.

seagull *Möwe*

Home. Home. Home is a house in a photograph, a pink house, pink as hollyhocks with lots of startled light. The man paints the walls of the apartment pink, but it's not the same, you know. She still sighs for her pink house, and then I think she cries. I would.

hollyhock *Malve*

Sometimes the man gets disgusted. He starts screaming and you can hear it all the way down the street.

Ay, she says, she is sad.

Oh, he says. Not again.

¿Cuándo, cuándo, cuándo? she asks.

¡Ay, caray! We *are* home. This *is* home. Here I am and here I stay. Speak English. Speak English. Christ!

cuándo (Span.) when
ay, caray (Span.) caramba

¡Ay! Mamacita, who does not belong, every once in a while lets out a cry, hysterical, high, as if he had torn the only skinny thread that kept her alive, the only road out to that country.

And then to break her heart forever, the baby boy, who has begun to talk, starts to sing the Pepsi commercial he heard on T.V.

No speak English, she says to the child who is singing in the language that sounds like tin. No speak English, no speak English, and bubbles into tears. No, no, no, as if she can't believe her ears.

T. Coraghessan Boyle, The Tortilla Curtain

In his novel, *The Tortilla Curtain,* Boyle describes the situation of a Mexican couple, illegal immigrants, trying to make a living in Southern California. Their discouraging efforts to find a home and a job run parallel to the sense of growing distrust and even xenophobia shown by middle-class Anglo society.

Cándido male hero of the novel

The excerpt presents Cándido's description of the situation of the illegal immigrants. Collect some of the most vivid examples.

América Cándido's wife
obscenity vulgar (sexual) directness
filth dirt
dumpster large container for trash

Cándido felt his jaws clench. What were they going to do now? If there was no work here anymore and *La Migra* to make sure of it, he and América would have to leave – either that or starve to death. That meant they'd have to go into the city, down to Santa Monica or Venice, or up over the canyon and into the Valley. That meant living on the streets, exposing América to the obscenity of the handout, the filth, the dumpsters out back of the supermarkets. And they were so close – another couple weeks of steady work and they could have had their apartment, could have established themselves, could have looked for work like human beings, riding the bus in freshly laundered clothes, seeking out the back rooms and sweatshops where nobody cared if you had documents or not. From there, in a year or two, they could have applied for their green cards – or maybe there would be another amnesty, who could tell? But now it was over. Now there was no more safe haven, no more camp in the woods. Now it was the streets.

to launder to clean
sweatshop illegal work place
green card permit to live and work in the US

In a daze, Cándido drifted away from the group gathered round the pickup, the weight of the news like a stone crushing his chest. Why not kill himself now and get it over with? He couldn't go back to Mexico, a country with forty percent unemployment and a million people a year entering the labor force, a country that was corrupt and bankrupt and so pinched by inflation that the farmers were burning their crops and nobody but the rich had enough to eat. He couldn't go back to his aunt, couldn't live off her again, butt of the entire village, couldn't face América's parents when he gave her back to them like some precious heirloom he'd borrowed and sullied. And he had a son coming, *un hijo,* the son he'd been yearning for since the day he'd met Resurrección, and what legacy did he have to leave him? Three hundred and twenty dollars in a peanut butter jar? A house of sticks even the prehistoric Indians would have rejected? A broken-down father who couldn't feed himself, let alone his family?

butt (fig.) behind

heirloom sth that has belonged to the family for generations
heir, heritage, to inherit, inheritance

to sully to stain
un hijo (Span.) a son
legacy what you leave as a gift before death
lead *Blei*
cipher secret, coded message

He staggered past the post office, his feet like lead, past the storefronts, the bright windows, the cars lined up like ciphers of the wealth that bloomed all around him, unattainable as the moon. And what was it all about? Work, that was all. The right to work, to have a job, earn your daily bread and a roof over your head. He was a criminal for daring to want it, daring to risk everything for the basic human necessities, and now even those were to be denied him. It stank. It did. These people, these *norteamericanos:* what gave them the right to all the riches of the world? He looked round him at the bustle in the lot of the Italian market, white faces, high heels, business suits, the greedy eyes and ravenous mouths. They lived in their glass palaces, with their gates and fences and security systems, they left half-eaten lobsters and beefsteaks on their plates when the rest of the world was starving, spent enough to feed and clothe a whole country on their exercise equipment, their swimming pools and tennis courts and jogging shoes, and all of them, even the poorest, had two cars. Where was the justice in that?

❶ Explain how Cándido characterises "these *norteamericanos*". Why does he choose to present his reproaches in the form of an interior monologue?

ravenous over-demanding

Abelardo Delgado, stupid america

Delgado's poem is about prejudices against the Chicanos in the United States. It transforms the current stereotypes and clichés among the Anglo majority against the Latino minority into poetic images. These in turn are Chicano idealisations and open to discussion.

The poem speaks in strong contrasts and antitheses. These denote how the Chicano thinks he is seen by the Anglo majority, on the one hand, and how he would like to be seen, on the other.

to carve to cut wood with great care
chicano popular term for Mexican
chicana, chicanito/a denoting Mexican origin
curse profane language
to flunk to fail

stupid america, see that chicano
with a big knife
in his steady hand
he doesn't want to knife you
he wants to sit on a bench
and carve christ figures
but you won't let him.
stupid america, hear that chicano
shouting curses on the street
he is a poet
without paper and pencil
and since he cannot write
he will explode.
stupid america, remember that chicanito
flunking math and english
he is the picasso
of your western states
but he will die
with one thousand masterpieces
hanging only from his mind.

Gloria Anzaldúa, To live in the Borderlands means you

The concrete everyday experience of thousands of her compatriots trying to cross the Mexican-American border illegally and the parallel existence of the Latino and Anglo cultures living side by side has influenced the topic of the poem and its formal and linguistic presentation. And above all the implied humanitarian and political message.

To live in the Borderlands means you
are neither *hispana india negra espanola*
ni gabacha, eres mestiza, mulata, half-breed
caught in the crossfire between camps
while carrying all five races on your back
not knowing which side to turn to, run from;

To live in the Borderlands means knowing
that the *india* in you, betrayed for 500 years,
is no longer speaking to you,
that *mexicanas* call you *rajetas,*
that denying the Anglo inside you
is as bad as having denied the Indian or Black;

Cuando vives en la frontera
people walk through you, the wind steals your voice,
you're a *burra, buey,* scapegoat,
forerunner of a new race,
half and half – both woman and man, neither –
a new gender;

To live in the Borderlands means to
put *chile* in the borscht,
eat whole wheat *tortillas,*
speak Tex-Mex with a Brooklyn accent;
be stopped by *la migra* at the border checkpoints;

Living in the Borderlands means you fight hard to
resist the gold elixir beckoning from the bottle,
the pull of the gun barrel,
the rope crushing the hollow of your throat;

In the Borderlands
you are the battleground
where enemies are kin to each other;
you are at home, a stranger,
the border disputes have been settled
the volley of shots have shattered the truce
you are wounded, lost in action
dead, fighting back;

To live in the Borderlands means
the mill with the razor white teeth wants to shred off
your olive-red skin, crush out the kernel, your heart
pound you pinch you roll you out
smelling like white bread but dead;

To survive the Borderlands
you must live *sin fronteras*
be a crossroads.

Make a list of what it means "to live in the Borderlands".

ni (Span.) neither
gabacha (Span.) Chicano term for a white woman
eres (Span.) you are
mestiza (Span.) mixed blood

rajetas (Span.) literally "split", i.e. having betrayed your word

cuando vives en la frontera (Span.) when you live in the border region
burra (Span.) donkey
buey (Span.) oxen
scapegoat sb blamed for sth he/she did not do

la migra (Span.) border patron

to beckon to call invitingly

kin related by blood

truce *Waffenstillstand*

sin fronteras (Span.) without borders

What is the function of the frequent use of Spanish words?

The colonial heritage: Multi-ethnicity in the United Kingdom

They are British after all: Immigrants from the Commonwealth

Hanif Kureishi, The Buddha of Suburbia

Immigrants are always emigrants, too. They live in two worlds or rather in between two worlds and tend to define themselves and what they do in terms of both their former home country and the country they live in now. In the case of the post-colonial relationship between India and England, this means that immigrants from India experience the clash between the English way of life (of the upper class) in India and the Indian way of life they feel condemned to by the "white" majority in England: Their whole existence seems to have been turned upside down.
The excerpt from the novel varies the intercultural theme. It shows two close friends, almost "brothers" from way back home, who try to adapt to the new situation. One does so by taking on English values and ways of life, the other one by retreating to Indian customs and even exploring new cultural and religious spheres, i.e. those of China.

Bombay Indian city, centre of "Bollywood"

What does this description reveal about the boys' former life-style in their native India?

Dad and Anwar lived next door to each other in Bombay and were best friends from the age of five. Dad's father, the doctor, had built a lovely low wooden house on Juhu beach for himself, his wife and his twelve children. Dad and Anwar would sleep on the veranda and at dawn run down to the sea and swim. They went to school in a horse-drawn rickshaw. At weekends they played cricket, and after school there was tennis on the family court. The servants would be ballboys. The cricket matches were often against the British, and you had to let them win. There were also constant riots and demonstrations and Hindu-Muslim fighting. You'd find your Hindu friends and neighbours chanting obscenities outside your house.

There were parties to go to, as Bombay was the home of the Indian film industry and one of Dad's elder brothers edited a movie magazine. Dad and Anwar loved to show off about all the film-stars they knew and the actresses they'd kissed. Once, when I was seven or eight, Dad told me he thought I should become an actor; it was a good life, he said, and the proportion of work to money was high. But really he wanted me to be a doctor, and the subject of acting was never mentioned again. At school the careers officer said I should go into Customs and Excise – obviously he thought I had a natural talent for scrutinizing suitcases. And Mum wanted me to go into the Navy, on the grounds, I think, that I liked wearing flared trousers.

Dad had had an idyllic childhood, and as he told me of his adventures with Anwar I often wondered why he'd condemned his own son to a dreary suburb of London of which it was said that when people drowned they saw not their lives but their double-glazing flashing before them.

It was only later, when he came to England, that Dad realized how complicated practical life could be. He'd never cooked before, never washed up, never cleaned his own shoes or made a bed. Servants did that. Dad told us that when he tried to remember the house in Bombay he could never visualize the kitchen: he'd never been in it. He remembered, though, that his favourite servant had been sacked for kitchen misdemeanours; once for making toast by lying on his back and suspending bread from between his toes over a flame, and on a second occasion for cleaning celery with a toothbrush – his own brush, as it happened, not the Master's, but that was no excuse. These incidents had made Dad a socialist, in so far as he was ever a socialist.

If Mum was irritated by Dad's aristocratic uselessness, she was also proud of his family. 'They're higher than the Churchills,' she said to people. 'He went to school in a horse-drawn carriage.' This ensured there would be no confusion between Dad and the swarms of Indian peasants who came to Britain in the 1950s and 1960s, and of whom it was said they were not familiar with cutlery and certainly not with toilets, since they squatted on the seats and shat from on high.

Unlike them, Dad was sent to England by his family to be educated. His mother knitted him and Anwar several itchy woollen vests and waved them off from Bombay, making them promise never to be pork-eaters. Like Gandhi and Jinnah before him, Dad would return to India a qualified and polished English gentleman lawyer and an accomplished ball-

careers officer sb to help students with their choice of career
to scrutinize to examine carefully

dreary grey and boring

double-glazing *Doppelverglasung*

➊ Compare life in England to that in India.

to sack to fire
misdemeanour a minor crime

cutlery knives, forks, spoons etc.

Gandhi Mahatma Gandhi (1869–1948), Indian political leader and social reformer
Jinnah Mohammed Ali Jinnah (1876–1948), Indian politician who founded the Islamic State of Pakistan

room dancer. But Dad had no idea when he set off that he'd never see his mother's face again. This was the great undiscussed grief of his life, and, I reckon, explained his helpless attachment to women who would take care of him, women he could love as he should have loved the mother to whom he never wrote a single letter.

London, the Old Kent Road, was a freezing shock to both of them. It was wet and foggy; people called you 'Sunny Jim'; there was never enough to eat, and Dad never took to dripping on toast. 'Nose drippings more like,' he'd say, pushing away the staple diet of the working class. 'I thought it would be roast beef and Yorkshire pudding all the way.' But rationing was still on, and the area was derelict after being bombed to rubble during the war. Dad was amazed and heartened by the sight of the British in England, though. He'd never seen the English in poverty, as roadsweepers, dustmen, shopkeepers and barmen. He'd never seen an Englishman stuffing bread into his mouth with his fingers, and no one had told him the English didn't wash regularly because the water was so cold – if they had water at all. And when Dad tried to discuss Byron in local pubs no one warned him that not every Englishman could read or that they didn't necessarily want tutoring by an Indian on the poetry of a pervert and a madman.

rationing limits on the amount of food for each person (during and after the war)

Byron Lord George Byron (1788–1824), English poet

Fortunately, Anwar and Dad had somewhere to stay, at Dr Lal's, a friend of Dad's father. Dr Lal was a monstrous Indian dentist who claimed to be a friend of Bertrand Russell. At Cambridge during the war, a lonely Russell advised Dr Lal that masturbation was the answer to sexual frustration. Russell's great discovery was a revelation to Dr Lal, who claimed to have been happy ever after. Was his liberation one of Russell's more striking achievements? For perhaps if Dr Lal hadn't been so forthright about sex with his two young and sexually rapacious lodgers, my father wouldn't have met my mother and I wouldn't be in love with Charlie.

Bertrand Russell (1872–1970) English philosopher and Nobel-Prize winner

forthright very open
rapacious greedy

Anwar was always plumper than Dad, with his podgy gut and round face. No sentence was complete without the flavouring of a few noxious words, and he loved the prostitutes who hung around Hyde Park. They called him Baby Face. He was less suave, too, for as soon as Dad's monthly allowance arrived from India, Dad visited Bond Street to buy bow-ties, bottle-green waistcoats and tartan socks, after which he'd have to borrow money from Baby Face. During the day Anwar studied aeronautical engineering in North London and Dad tried to glue his eyes to his law books. At night they slept in Dr Lal's consulting room among the dental equipment, Anwar sleep-

podgy fat
gut belly

noxious bad, hostile

bow-tie *Fliege*

ing in the chair itself. One night, enraged by the mice running around him, by sexual frustration too, and burning with the itching of his mother's woollen vests, Dad dressed himself in Lal's pale blue smock, picked up the most ferocious drill and attacked Anwar as he slept. Anwar screamed when he awoke to find the future guru of Chislehurst coming at him with a dentist's drill. This playfulness, this refusal to take anything seriously, as if life didn't matter, characterized Dad's attitude to his studies. Dad just couldn't concentrate. He'd never worked before and it didn't suit him now. Anwar started to say of Dad, 'Haroon is called to the Bar every day – at twelve o'clock and five-thirty.'

Dad defended himself: 'I go to the pub to think.'

'No, not think – drink,' Anwar replied.

On Fridays and Saturdays they went to dances and smooched blissfully to Glenn Miller and Count Basie and Louis Armstrong. That is where Dad first laid eyes and hands on a pretty working-class girl from the suburbs called Margaret. My mother told me that she loved him, her little man, from the first moment she saw him. He was sweet and kind and utterly lost-looking, which made women attempt to make him found-looking.

There was a friend of Mum's whom Baby Face walked out with, and apparently even walked in with, but Anwar was already married, to Jeeta, a princess whose family came on horseback to the wedding held in the old British hill station of Murree, in the north of Pakistan. Jeeta's brothers carried guns, which made Anwar nervous and want to head for England.

Soon Princess Jeeta joined Anwar in England, and she became Auntie Jeeta to me. Auntie Jeeta looked nothing like a princess, and I mocked her because she couldn't speak English properly. She was very shy and they lived in one dirty room in Brixton. It was no palace and it backed on to the railway line. One day Anwar made a serious mistake in the betting shop and won a lot of money. He bought a short lease on a toy shop in South London. It was a miserable failure until Princess Jeeta made him turn it into a grocer's shop. They were set up. Customers flocked.

In contrast, Dad was going nowhere. His family cut off his money when they discovered from a spy – Dr Lal – that he was being called to the Bar only to drink several pints of rough stout and brown ale wearing a silk bow-tie and a green waistcoat. Dad ended up working as a clerk in the Civil Service for £3 a week. His life, once a cool river of balmy distraction, of beaches and cricket, of mocking the British, and dentists' chairs, was

guru of Chislehurst reference to the narrator's father as the Buddha of Suburbia (title of novel)

to be called to the Bar *Berufung an ein höheres Gericht,* here: play on words with bar meaning "pub"

to smooch to kiss

to mock to make fun of

to flock to arrive in large numbers

stout dark beer

➊ Sketch the contrasting worlds of India and England.

now a cage of umbrellas and steely regularity. It was all trains and shitting sons, and the bursting of frozen pipes in January, and the lighting of coal fires at seven in the morning: the organization of love into suburban family life in a two-up-two-down semi-detached in South London. Life was thrashing him for being a child, an innocent who'd never had to do anything for himself. Once when I was left with him all day and I shat myself, he was bewildered. He stood me naked in the bath while he fetched a cup from which, standing on the other side of the bathroom as if I had the plague, he threw water at my legs while holding his nose with his other hand.

semi-detached *Doppelhaushälfte*

bewildered not knowing what to do

I don't know how it all started, but when I was ten or eleven he turned to Lieh Tzu, Lao Tzu and Chuang Tzu as if they'd never been read before, as if they'd been writing exclusively for him.

Lieh Tzu, Lao Tzu and Chuang Tzu Chinese philosophers

We continued to visit Baby Face and Princess Jeeta on Sunday afternoons, the only time the shop closed. Dad's friendship with Anwar was still essentially a jokey one, a cricket-, boxing-, athletics-, tennis-watching one. When Dad went there with a library copy of *The Secret of the Golden Flower* Anwar snatched it from him, held it up and laughed.

'What's this bloody-fool thing you're playing with now?'

Dad promptly started up with, 'Anwar, *yaar,* you don't realize the great secrets I'm uncovering! How happy I feel now I'm understanding life at last!'

Anwar interrupted, stabbing at Dad with his roll-up. 'You bloody Chinese fool. How are you reading rubbish when I'm making money! I've paid off my bastard mortgage!'

mortgage *Hypothek*

Dad was so keen for Anwar to understand that his knees were vibrating. 'I don't care about money. There's always money. I must understand these secret things.'

Anwar raised his eyes to heaven and looked at Mum, who sat there, bored. They both had sympathy for Dad, and loved him, but in these moods love was mixed with pity, as if he were making some tragic mistake, like joining the Jehovah's Witnesses. The more he talked of the Yin and Yang, cosmic consciousness, Chinese philosophy, and the following of the Way, the more lost Mum became. He seemed to be drifting away into outer space, leaving her behind; she was a suburban woman, quiet and kind, and found life with two children and Dad difficult enough as it was. There was at the same time a good chunk of pride in Dad's Oriental discoveries, which led him to denigrate Anwar's life.

Yin and Yang the principle of essential opposites in nature such as female and male

Way main work of Lao Tse, 600 BC

chunk a large piece

to denigrate to speak badly about

'You're only interested in toilet rolls, sardine tins, sanitary pads and turnips,' he told Anwar. 'But there are many more things, *yaar,* in heaven and earth, than you damn well dream of in Penge.'

'I haven't got time to dream!' interrupted Anwar. 'Nor should you be dreaming. Wake up! What about getting some promotion so Margaret can wear some nice clothes. You know what women are like, *yaar.'*

'The whites will never promote us,' Dad said. 'Not an Indian while there is a white man left on the earth. You don't have to deal with them – they still think they have an Empire when they don't have two pennies to rub together.'

Meera Syal, Anita and Me

The excerpt has been taken from Meera Syal's debut novel in which she describes, seen through the eyes of a girl-narrator, the difficult phases of a teenage girl growing up in a little English town that is so far away from her native Punjabi and India. The autobiographically-based novel focuses on the typical immigrant experience of having to cope with so many differences and oppositions simultaneously: two countries and two nations as well as two opposite cultures and traditions. Meena, the girl-narrator, closely observes and comments on what is going on around her in the little English community of Tollington as a whole, in her immediate neighbourhood, her peer group with Anita and of course during family visits.

Whenever my father got sick of our three-up-three-down with its high uneven walls and narrow winding stairs, sick of the damp in the pantry, the outside toilet, the three buses it took to get to work, taking a bath in our bike shed and having to whisper when he wanted to shout, he'd turn to my mother and say, 'You wanted this house, remember that.'

My mother grew up in a small Punjabi village not far from Chandigarh. As she chopped onions for the evening meal or scrubbed the shine back onto a steel pan or watched the clouds of curds form in a bowl of slowly setting homemade yoghurt, any action with a rhythm, she would begin a mantra about her ancestral home. She would chant of a three-storeyed flat-roofed house, blinkered with carved wooden shutters around a dust yard where an old-fashioned pump stood under a mango tree. She would talk of running with her tin mug to the she-goat tethered to the tree and, holding the mug under its nipples,

➊ Look for differences and opposites in the description of the narrator's experience. Can you detect any kind of pattern?

pantry small room for provisions
Punjabi belonging to Punjab, formerly Brit. NW India, now an independent state
to chop to slice into small pieces
curd *Dickmilch, Quark*
mantra sacred sayings in Hinduism and Buddhism
ancestral belonging to parents or forefathers
to chant to sing; here: to speak in praise
to carve to cut from wood
to tether to tie with a rope

orchard large group of fruit trees
peacock *Pfau*
keening lamenting

What does the new modern home mean to some immigrants as opposed to Meena's mother?

to preen to congratulate o.s.
amenities facilities such as schools, public transport etc.
lavvy (ifml) lavatory

apology excuse, here: poor example of
to apologise, apologetic

to protrude to stick out
crease *Bügelfalte*

salwar kameez (Ind.) ornamented Indian dress

incarnation coming to life

incredulity inability to believe
bewilderment utter astonishment

to stab to strike with a knife
partition division (of countries)
riot rebellion, uproar
to stalk to follow secretly and aggressively
ravenous greedy

pulling down a foaming jet of milk straight into her father's morning tea. She spoke of the cobra who lived in the damp grasses beneath the fallen apples in the vast walled orchard, of the peacocks whose keening kept her awake on rainy monsoon nights, of her Muslim neighbours whom they always made a point of visiting on festivals, bringing sweetmeats to emphasise how the land they shared was more important than the religious differences that would soon tear the Punjab in two.

Yet, in England, when all my mother's friends made the transition from relatives' spare rooms and furnished lodgings to homes of their own, they all looked for something 'modern'. 'It's really up-to-date, Daljit,' one of the Aunties would preen as she gave us the grand tour of her first proper home in England. 'Look, extra strong flush system ... Can opener on the wall ... Two minutes walk to all local amenities ...' But my mother knew what she wanted. When she stepped off the bus in Tollington, she did not see the outside lavvy or the apology for a garden or the medieval kitchen, she saw fields and trees, light and space, and a horizon that welcomed the sky which, on a warm night and through squinted eyes, could almost look something like home.

At first I would listen entranced to this litany of love, imagining my mother as I had seen her in those crumpled black and white photographs hoarded in a shiny suitcase on top of her wardrobe. She was skinny and dark then, all eyes and stick insect limbs protruding from a white pyjama suit with paper-sharp creases in the legs. She retained this image, of a country girl lost in the big city, throughout her teens and early twenties, only the costume changed. Here was mama in a school play, a coat hanger for a home-sewn robe, mama winning a race as All Delhi College Champion, running in full length *salwar kameez*, mama as a lecturer, standing in front of a class of bored Delhi teenage girls, looking younger than all of them. On paper her achievements were remarkably impressive – actress, athlete, teacher – incarnations from other lives, trumpeting talents I would never see fully realised. But I still found it comforting that in every face she wore, I still saw the incredulity and bewilderment she so often turned on me. I liked knowing I could still surprise my mother.

But gradually I got bored, and then jealous of this past that excluded me; she had milked goats, stroked peacocks, pulled sugar cane from the earth as a mid-morning snack. She had even seen someone stabbed to death, much later on when the family had moved to Delhi and partition riots stalked the streets like a ravenous animal. A man in a rickshaw, she said.

The driver gave him a *bidi,* took one himself and indicated he needed a light. As the customer fumbled in the pockets of his ill-fitting suit (and this memory seemed to upset her greatly, remembering how his shirt sleeves protruded from worn linen elbows), the driver reached into his *dhoti* and brought out a knife which he plunged into his fellow smoker's head, a lit match still in his victim's twitching hand.
That was my favourite, but she would not repeat it more than twice. The last time I had asked her to tell me the Rickshaw Story, she looked at me much as I imagine Damien's mother looked when she gave her smiling baby his first shampoo and found three sixes curled up like commas behind his tiny pink ear. But the story did not fascinate me because of the violence, what obsessed me was this meeting of two worlds, the collision of the epic with the banal. A shared cigarette and a hidden knife, a too-small suit, probably borrowed from a brother who was expecting it back that evening, and a bloody betrayal. I listened to this tale and heard huge boulders moving somewhere, my centre of gravity shifted and I saw the breath of monsters gathering on the horizon. Terrible things could happen, even to ordinary people like me, and they were always unplanned.

bidi (Ind.) cigarette

dhoti (Ind.) man's dress

Explain what the narrator means by the "collision of the epic with the banal".

betrayal disclosing a secret, breaking a promise
to betray, betrayer

boulder large stone

Atima Srivastava, Looking for Maya

In her first novel, Bombay- (Mumbai-) born Atima Srivastava introduces Mira, a young Hindu woman living in London. She has just graduated from university and has completed her first literary work for which she has won a prize. She is in love with Luke, an English music student who has been awarded a grant to study in India. This excerpt is about Mira's meeting with Luke's father Ralph and his friend Amrit, an established English writer, who like Mira is of Indian origin.

'And how are you, Mira? How are things with you?' said Ralph, leaning across to me with a genial smile.
I shrugged. 'OK, I haven't done much about anything. I suppose I should think about getting a job.'
'You must talk to Amrit,' said Ralph suddenly. 'He's a writer too.'
I cringed. I had won a short-story competition some months ago, won a hundred pounds, blown it on a weekend to Spain

How does the narrator make the reader aware of the more subtle forms of cultural diversity?

to cringe to draw back due to sth unpleasant

RaviKavi Mira's parents
degree academic title
to dismiss here: not to value
to belch here: to speak bitterly
itinerary travel plan or route
Punjabi belonging to Punjab, formerly NW Brit. India, now an independent state
Bengali person living in Bengal or in Bangladesh, mostly Hindu
reminiscent making one think of

Collect information on the Indian caste system.

scribe clerk
to imbibe to take in
kinship close relation

with Luke, who had boasted to everybody about his girlfriend the writer. RaviKavi had smiled knowingly on the phone. Of course I was going to be a writer eventually, despite the degree in History; it was in our genes. Never mind that RaviKavi hadn't written for twenty years, left their literary friends behind in Delhi and Bombay, lost all the books they had published, dismissed the mark they had each made on the landscape of Hindi poetry.

'Oh, god, it's nothing. Nothing really. Of no consequence,' I said with embarrassment as Luke and Ralph explained.

'All writers begin from no consequences,' grinned Amrit.

'Mira's parents are both poets,' said Ralph proudly, even though he had never met my parents, never heard them reciting their poems about rural India and democracy and open skies to the Visiting Gods who stayed in the house and belched their way through the London itineraries prepared by my parents.

'Really?' said Amrit turning towards me. 'What are their names?'

I smiled. It was such an Indian question. English people asked your name out of politeness and necessity, but for an Indian your surname signified everything they needed to know about where you came from, what sort of background, even what your profession was. When I was growing up, the stubborn point in our little triangular family, I used to think Indian people walked about with maps rolled up under their arms, ready to pinpoint each other, label them and talk of them, in the stereotypes they had unearthed. Arrey, he is a Gujju, don't expect a discount ... Delhi has full-eee degenerated under this pushy Punjabi culture ... of course he is a scholar, Bengalis have always been ...

Amrit hadn't heard of Ravi Chowdhary or Kavita Joshi, but he nodded just the same, and I was aware that I wanted to tell him, wanted him to know where I was from, which meant explaining where RaviKavi were from. He knew Lucknow, how civilized the people were in that small town where my parents had grown up speaking that gorgeous language referred to as Hindustani, the mix of Urdu and Hindi reminiscent of the Nawabs of Oudh.

'You know what they say about Kayastas?' said Amrit with a smile. 'This caste you belong to, the writers' caste. This odd fifth caste. They began as scribes in the Mughal empire and imbibed the ways of the Muslims. My father used to say, never trust a Kayasta, they are sharaabi kebabis. They drink and eat meat, they are nearly Muslims themselves!'

We all burst out laughing and I felt an odd kinship with him because he knew these things.

'I thought Muslims didn't drink?' said Luke ingenuously.

'They're not supposed to drink,' I said shyly. 'But their music and literature ...'

'Hindus are a pious lot,' declared Amrit and smiled.

'The fifth caste?' asked Luke in puzzlement.

'See, they are neither priests, nor warriors, nor merchants. Nor are they the "Children of God",' Amrit smiled. 'They are side-ys.'

I laughed out loud at his use of the euphemism for Untouchability, at his use of Bollywood slang for hooligans.

'But surely,' insisted Luke, 'the caste system isn't relevant any more? Not amongst educated, urban people?'

'Indeed, indeed,' said Amrit, with such a show of innocence, that I wanted to laugh again.

He didn't have intimate knowledge of the world of Hindi literature but he knew how I had learnt my language, from the privileged position of the daughter of poets amongst traders and clerks and bank managers. He knew in the way, I realized with a sudden shock, Luke or Ralph would never know. His Hindi pronunciation was accented. He must be an English writer, I remember thinking.

'And your parents, do they live here too?' asked Amrit.

'They've gone back to India, because my grandad died and my dad had to sort out the house and then they went to Delhi because they're trying to build a house there on a plot they bought years ago,' I said in a rush.

I wondered if he knew automatically the freedom enshrined in those words. If he could imagine how my heart had soared at their worried faces at Terminal 3, when they were leaving me behind, all alone, unheard of, free as a bird. How I had reassured them that I would be fine, I would look in on their house regularly, I would manage very well in the flat they had recently purchased in an uncharacteristic burst of investment. I would thrive on the monthly allowance they had arranged with my bank. RaviKavi had never planned their lives, looked down their noses at money. They had moved from their small town to big cities but always lived frugally, enjoying their own community of two, never making any real friends in this country, inviting all the old ones to come and complete and redraw the circle of Delhi-Bombay-London.

'I've been living independently for nearly three years anyway, Dad, what's the problem?' I'd said confidently and RaviKavi had frowned at each other.

'We'll speak every week. You keep all your doors locked. We'll be back soon,' my dad had threatened me. 'Soon' had turned

ingenuous naive, innocent

pious strongly religious

Bollywood Bombay as centre of Indian film industry, Indian Hollywood

➜ Can you explain?

plot a small piece of land

to thrive to live well, to prosper

to look down one's nose at to disapprove

frugal avoiding waste, esp. with money

to abandon to leave alone

aerogramme airmail

into months, because land plots couldn't be abandoned, building work couldn't be left unsupervised in Delhi, which was lawless these days, so their blue aerogrammes had explained.

'Take as long as you want,' I'd said generously, already seeing my brilliant future spreading before me like a glittering universe.

'Don't be funny,' my mother had admonished.

What do the rules and the ➊ patterns of behaviour show?

archaic old-fashioned

to regale to entertain

RaviKavi hadn't any need to say don't do anything to excess, don't be a bad girl, don't make us ashamed of you. Lucknow people didn't speak directly, it was vulgar. In the Mughal times, the pattern of conversation had been full of incredible politenesses, delightfully archaic phrases that my father had often regaled me with. When the cultured Muslims went to enquire after a friend's health, they didn't rudely ask, 'Are you unwell?' They would say, 'I hear those who wish you ill, are unwell.'

'Ralph tells me you're off to foreign parts?' said Amrit, neatly changing the subject from me to Luke and I was glad of it.

elation great happiness

naff (ifml) lacking in style

to snog to kiss

permissiveness freedom to do whatever one wants

sensibility feeling about what is morally right

'I'm planning a trip to India,' said Luke enthusiastically, absently slipping his hand across the table over mine. I couldn't help feeling a mixture of elation and embarrassment whenever Luke demonstrated affection towards me in front of either of his parents. They had thought nothing of Luke and me sleeping together in the spare room in their house in Brighton, twenty minutes from the front. Somehow, despite his Englishness, I was conscious of Amrit's eyes upon us, just like I had always been fearful of 'uncles' and 'aunties' roaming the Pizza Parades and Chix Chox of my childhood in North London. Any boys I knew then had been strictly instructed by me that kissing and cuddling was naff in public. I had yearned to snog on pavements, suck tongues on the bus, but the humiliation of my parents' certain disappointment had been too much to bear. University had been the site of permissiveness, safely sixty miles from uncles and aunties and Lucknow sensibilities.

'Luke's researching the musical influences of the East upon the Western tradition,' said Ralph, and Amrit raised his eyebrows.

'I'm waiting for a grant from the Arts Council, it should be enough for a few months,' said Luke. 'There's an international artists' community on the edge of Delhi. It's a sort of cultural centre, multi-disciplined. I want to go and stay there.'

John Agard, Oxford Don

The two poems of the Caribbean author deal with the central themes of his life and his work, namely the inseparable unity of language and history and his own personal, cultural and national identity.

Me not no Oxford don
me a simple immigrant
from Clapham Common
I didn't graduate
I immigrate

But listen Mr. Oxford don
I'm a man on de run
and a man on de run
is a dangerous one

I ent have no gun
I ent have no knife
but mugging de Queen's English
is the story of my life

I don't need no axe
to split up yu syntax
I don't need no hammer
to mash up yu grammar

I warning you Mr. Oxford don
I'm a wanted man
and a wanted man
is a dangerous one

Dem accuse me of assault
on de Oxford dictionary
imagin a concise peaceful man like me
dem want me to serve time
for inciting rhyme to riot
but I tekking it quiet
down here in Clapham Common

I'm not violent man Mr. Oxford don
I only armed wit muh human breath
but human breath
is a dangerous weapon

don professor

Clapham Common London district

to graduate to finish university

Immigrants as a rule have problems with the language. How is this topic treated in the poem?

to mug to attack, to rob

to mash to beat, to crush

assault attack

concise brief and to the point

to serve time to go to jail

to incite to provoke

riot revolt

So mek dem send one big word after me
I ent serving no jail sentence
I slashing suffix in self-defence
I bashing future with present tense
and if necessary

I making de Queen's English accessory to my offence

to slash to cut
suffix attachment to the stem of a word
to bash to strike
accessory to involved in

John Agard, checking out me history

Make a list of the different historical references. Then use the Internet for detailed information and finally show the importance of history for a person's sense of identity (Caribbean/Haitian/Jamaican/English/American).

Dem tell me
Dem tell me
Wha dem want fo tell me

Bandage up me eye with me own history
Blind me to me own identity

Dem tell me bout 1066 and all dat
Dem tell me bout Dick Whittington and he cat
But Toussaint L'Ouverture
no dem never tell me bout dat

Toussaint
a slave
with vision
lick back
Napoleon
battalion
and first Black

Republic born
Toussaint de thorn
to de French
Toussaint de beacon
of de Haitian Revolution

Dem tell me bout de man who discover de balloon
and de cow who jump over de moon

Dem tell me bout de dish ran away with the spoon
but dem never tell me bout Nanny de maroon

Nanny
see-far woman
of mountain dream
fire-woman struggle
hopeful stream
to freedom river

Dem tell me bout Lord Nelson and Waterloo
but dem never tell me bout Shaka de great Zulu
Dem tell me bout Columbus and 1492
but what happen to de Caribs and de Arawaks too

Dem tell me bout Florence Nightingale and she lamp
and how Robin Hood used to camp
Dem tell me bout old King Cole was a merry old soul
but dem never tell me bout Mary Seacole

From Jamaica
she travel far
to the Crimean War

she volunteer to go
and even when de British said no
she still brave the Russian snow
a healing star
among the wounded
a yellow sunrise
to the dying

Dem tell me
Dem tell me wha dem want fo tell me
But now I checking out me own history
I carving out me identity.

Multi-ethnicity: A global phenomenon

Multi-ethnicity: Not a one-way road

Anchee Min, Katherine

Katherine, a young American, goes to Shanghai to teach English. There, she is confronted with Chinese men and women whose wish to learn the foreign language is also stimulated by the desire to learn about a strange though fascinating culture which is contrary to that of Communist, post-Mao China. Zebra, the young female narrator, makes friends with the American and becomes her confidante and guide in Chinese ways, just as much as Katherine becomes her tutor in the American way of life. With two women in a crucial dialogue, it goes without saying that femininity is at stake. The dialogue also shows the radically different social conditions in which both women have grown up in their respective countries.

coffin box for a dead person

cot a small, canvas bed

surgery medical operation

That night I thought again of my father's life in jail. Of his solitary cell, no larger than a coffin, a small opening the only source of light and air. How it was impossible to stand up, how he lay on the bare concrete without a cot, how he was defenseless against the winter, how his joints were slowly destroyed. Twenty years of longing, every waking minute wondering how his wife and children were. Twenty years of severe loneliness. The Party believed "loneliness was the scalpel one used to perform surgery on the soul." My father relied on his imagination to survive.

How can the experience of hatred stimulate an understanding of love?

Unlike Lion Head, I felt I knew love because I had experienced enough hatred. I knew what it was like to miss a dear person like my father as a child. I knew what it was like to sit on the corner, dreaming of greeting my father as he gets off the bus. I learned that the cruelty of winter teaches one to appreciate the warmth of spring – unbearable summer, the coolness of autumn.

I visited Katherine early one evening to look over her Chinese composition. It was an excuse to see her. She never mentioned paying me money again; perhaps she understood she could pay me back with her attention.

I found Katherine interesting no matter what she said or did. I collected in my mind the comments she dropped. She said amazing things that I had never thought of, like, "Give voice to your deepest and most immediate emotion." She would explain and explain until I understood what she meant. In this case she said she had been talking about the kind of emotion that existed in poems and that responded only to the thoughts and sensations that gave birth to poems.

Sometimes I could not follow her at all, but I would keep listening to her. I was in rapture, for she stimulated me in such an unfamiliar way. I watched her when she spoke. Sometimes I felt like I was dreaming. She was my window, and through its frame, I saw another world.

She laughed with such directness. When she learned that I was embarrassed about what happened with Lion Head at Wolf Teeth, she laughed. She kept saying to me, "Look, you are twenty-nine years old. If you were in America, you'd probably have been married and divorced by now. Big deal."

"No, no, no," I said. "You have missed my point ..." I tried to explain. "You must understand the differences between East and West."

She said, "Oh, come on, underneath it all, people are the same."

She said that I was a nut, that Chinese were nuts in a lot of ways. "You're driving me crazy, and unfortunately I like it," she said, smoothing her hair with her hand. "You want to know something? I think you are wild. Just like me. Nobody can really tie you down. You know, you don't live with the foot-binding cloth anymore."

I looked at her. I nodded. I found her so beautiful. I wanted to be like her.

She laid out my thoughts for me. She was a sickle and I a rake. I was amazed at her logic, the way she tallied her thoughts, pro and con, on a piece of paper with a pencil, how she made decisions. She said life was a process of making choices. One had to prepare for the inevitable deaths that came with change. She asked me to remember that there would be no choice that did not mean loss. She liked to sing, "You gotta win a little, lose a little ..."

She made me learn from myself. She turned me into a sponge. I sucked the water of her knowledge. She told me that in

rapture extreme excitement

➔ This is a "transcultural" viewpoint. Does it do justice to cultural interaction?

nuts (ifml) totally crazy

sickle curved blade for cutting long grass

rake instrument used to gather hay, leaves etc.

to tally here: to present

sponge *Schwamm*

What is the popularity of psychotherapy meant to say about the US society?

America there were many psychotherapists, people who earned a living by discussing with people whatever was on their minds. "It's very expensive. Yet many Americans can't do without it. The more they pay, the better they feel. Some people believe the only way they'll be cured is if they pay too much."

Are humour and wit something specific to a particular culture or a region?

Looking at my confused expression, she said: "Gee, you're so serious, you don't get my jokes at all, do you? That scares me, because I can't help kidding around. If you can't tell what's a joke and what's not, you'll be all messed up. Talk to me, don't give me that bull's face."

Katherine told me her secret wish was to adopt a child. I had a hard time comprehending her. I sat on her bed and looked at her. I had just finished telling her a story of a village family in my aunt's province who'd abandoned their baby just because it was a girl child. Katherine was in tears. "How could any parent possibly have the heart to do that?"

Katherine made me want to ignore her. She did not know that this type of story was not news to me. It happened in China too often. Katherine refused to accept reality. I told her that she was drowning herself in other people's tragedy. She went silent. I saw her fury.

lynx *Luchs*

"You are cold," she said to me. "Cruel, you people." Her lynx eyes opened wide in anger, her pupils became big question marks.

petal *Blumenblatt*

to paralyze to make unable to move
paralysis, paralytic

I don't know how it happened, but at that moment, my heart felt a sudden tenderness. Her way of thinking touched me. It was something I had forgotten or maybe had never known. She unfolded the petals of my dry heart. A flower I did not know existed began to bloom inside me. It had been too long that my spirit had been paralyzed. I couldn't recall when I stopped feeling for my own people. Katherine stretched my life beyond its own circumstance. It was the kind of purity she preserved that moved me. She had a child's power. She pinned me to the wall and incited a revolution in my heart.

to incite to set in motion

paddy (rice) field

We sat by the window in her hut, facing the rice paddies. Watching farmers spread pig shit with their hands, listening to them curse the weather and the animals.

How can history and circumstance condition your view of the world?

I told Katherine that I had always believed that circumstance made me who I was and I believed firmly that humans were born evil. I believed it was a universal truth because I lived through it. Survivors were people who took only what was useful for the moment and abandoned the rest. They refused to understand shame. Did the parents who abandoned their infant feel ashamed? They got rid of that baby just like they got rid of pus on their faces. They thought the pain was worth enduring. Hope was reborn when they laid the sleeping infant on the village road. They refused to hear her cries. They believed that when the sun rose everything would be forgotten. That was my China, not Katherine's.

pus *Eiter*

I began to cry. Katherine was shocked at how emotional I'd become. She did not know what to do.

I told her that I did not appreciate her sentimentality. "You American, you lived a sugary life. What do you know about survival? Starving kids steal, cheat, and murder – they will do anything to fill their stomachs. This was my life. I gave up trying to reconcile with fate. It was not a baby I killed – it was me! Me!"

to reconcile to bring o.s. to accept

Katherine looked at me; slowly her eyes became gentle. She sat down beside me and took my hands in hers. She hugged me and I felt her tears on my cheek.

"I was seduced and raped," I began. I told her about my Party boss at Elephant Fields, Mr. Kee, a man of sixty. He tortured me when I started working there. He assigned me to the most dangerous jobs. After a year he called me in and told me that he was removing me from the fields and making me his personal secretary. He took me to Party meetings and would touch me while we rode on tractors. He promised that he would send me back to Shanghai if I let him have his way with me. I was just twenty and far from home, but I didn't want to sell myself.

Mr. Kee sent me back to the fields to work with dynamite. I witnessed several fatal accidents on the job and I began to feel very scared. Mr. Kee invited me to a peasant's house during the Chinese New Year to "talk about my future." The peasant was a blind man. We sat on a big clay platform that was both the table and the bed. The house was lit with candles. I drank the wine Mr. Kee offered and I passed out shortly after. He had put drugs in the drink. Before I realized what was happening, I was raped. I could feel him undressing me, but I had no strength to move my limbs or make a sound. I lost consciousness. When I woke up, Mr. Kee was gone and the blind man said that there had never been anyone but me in his house.

fatal causing death

I confronted Mr. Kee. He was eating dinner with his wife and family celebrating New Year's Eve. Wiping his oily mouth, he said he didn't know what I was talking about. He said that he had no such meeting with me. He accused me of insulting him and trying to ruin his reputation.

"Don't try to pull a hair from a tiger's head," he warned me.

Interpret Zebra's reaction to abortion in the light of Chinese overpopulation and the one-(male) child-policy.

I missed my period for two months, I couldn't stand the idea of being pregnant with Mr. Kee's beast inside me. I was too ashamed to go to a doctor. In China, any woman who got pregnant before marriage destroyed her future. I didn't know what to do about my growing belly. I ran, jumped, drank dirty water, worked overtime trying to get rid of it. But still I could not stop the little heart from beating. Mr. Kee saw what was happening and took me to see a relative of his who was a village witch. She made me drink Chinese medicine to poison the fetus.

reed long grass near water

The moment I drank down the medicine I realized that I would never be able to escape this fate. I was a mother who was murdering her child minute by minute. After work one day, I went to lie in the wild reeds. It was a cloudy and windy evening. I began talking to my dying baby. I asked for its forgiveness. I said I could not imagine what it felt like to have such a mother. I cried because it was too late, I had already taken the medicine. I tried not to think about which part of its body the poison had reached. I couldn't help but envision the process of deformation, I could see the medicine chewing up the heart, the limbs, the brain. I felt its struggle for life. I screamed up at God, asking why I was made to do this.

Three months old. Was it a girl or a boy? I felt part of me dying with it. I touched my swelling breasts. I thought she or he would never have my milk. The witch had told me about other women with unwanted children she had received. Most of them took her prescription and killed the fetus, but a few had delivered deformed babies. She gave me the address of an orphanage and told me to drop the baby secretly at night if I failed to abort it. Would the fetus die from the poison or come through me deformed? Every moment I wished for it to die. My mind was at the point of bursting.

Two weeks later, as I was pushing a cart filled with stones, I felt a warm stream gush out of my bottom parts. I ran toward the bushes. I could feel blood dripping down my legs. I hid myself in the bushes, I squatted down, and a bloody tissue dropped. It looked like a fish, a black-red fish. It was my half-formed baby.

I broke down. I couldn't touch it. I took off my blouse and tried to stop the blood from running. My hands were soaked in blood. I had no tears. My breath was short. I heard dynamite explode nearby as the world turned upside down. I fainted.

I woke up. It was early evening. I wanted to bury the "fish" but I had no strentgh. I laid reeds on top of it and ran away from it with all my might.

might strength

Katherine tightened her arms around my shoulders. She stroked my back tenderly. Holding her, I fell asleep in exhaustion. Katherine stayed up all night.

exhaustion state of being very tired

I woke at dawn. Katherine was outside, sitting on a wooden stool, writing in her notebook. I walked toward her and she asked how I felt. I told her that every time I thought of Elephant Fields I despised life and hated the world.

Katherine gazed at me in the rising sunlight. "I don't know how to make you see life in another way. It's possible that we can never truly understand each other. But this is what I always say to myself in rough times: Life is not about giving up after a string of disappointments. Giving up is much easier than carrying on.

"Because my biological mother was blind and deaf, I used to think I might become blind and deaf at any moment. I still don't want to take the risk if there is even the slightest chance that a child of mine could turn out to be blind or deaf. But I don't allow myself to be bitter. I don't think life is unfair. We have this saying in America, it's actually a cliché: 'A pessimist sees a glass half-empty, an optimist sees it half-full.' It all depends on how you look at things. You see what I'm saying?"

How does the little anecdote illustrate the very American creed, the basis of American optimism?

I sat down next to Katherine. She handed me her notebook. I turned the pages. I couldn't read her flying handwriting. I turned to face her. She was in her brown sweater; her face was pale. She was looking at the sun.

Our two lives merged. I thought, Katherine who had every reason in the world to be cruel and cynical, who could have been a thief, a robber, a cheater, a drug user, a murderer, chose not to be. I saw how her spirit won out over fate. She woke me from my world of nightmares and brought me into the world of hope. She took away my bitterness, and a new mind began to take shape in me, a mind both wild and tame.

to merge to blend together

tame opposite of wild

At the edge of the rice paddies, the sun jumped over the gray horizon like a giant fireball. I reached out for her. Without turning her head, she took my hands in hers. *"Tai-yang-nee-zao!"* – Good morning, Sunshine! she said, smiling, with tears glittering in her eyes.

paddy field

Norman Williams, Protest

The Canadian playwright's short play is set in 1900. It is about the encounter of two different cultures, those of the East and the West, which are personified in the father in his forties and the daughter, aged 17. In this scene, the daughter's introduction of a Western chair into her Japanese parents' home is used as a pretext to present values and customs of the older generation that are being questioned by the daughter. Several examples of how life in Japan has changed are given before the central topic, that of arranged marriage, is raised.

Sitting and taking a seat also have ceremonial implications. For further reference see the cartoon on the assessment page, p. 132.

on the verge of just about to

Ishimoto name of teacher and tutor

sash cloth worn for decoration

What do you get to know about the different appreciation of the Japanese tradition of learning and teaching?

FATHER: It's not a very comfortable chair, is it?

DAUGHTER: *We* aren't used to sitting in chairs.

FATHER: That is true. Still, I have done so before. *(The daughter shows interest.)* In the big cities they are quite commonly seen. But they aren't plain wooden ones like this. Some of them I have seen are made of shining brown cowhide; cool to the touch and so slippery I would be afraid to sit in one. Others are huge affairs with springs in the seat, and when you sit down it would seem you are sinking into a deep, soft cloud. I imagine the Westerners use them for sleeping. At least the ones I saw seated in them seemed on the verge of sleep.

DAUGHTER: Oh, there are so many things I have *never* seen.

FATHER: That is true of most of us, and many of the things we never see are right before our eyes all the time.

DAUGHTER: I didn't mean *those* things. I mean the new, wonderful things the Westerners have.

FATHER: *(Rises and takes the chair out, left.)* I will put this into the "shoe-off" room; it disturbs your grandmother.

DAUGHTER: And may I keep it in my room?

FATHER: We will have to think about that.

DAUGHTER: Ishimoto said it was a very fine chair and that houses in America had twenty or thirty each in them.

FATHER: *(Returns from left.)* So it was Ishimoto who gave you the chair? I guessed it was.

DAUGHTER: He didn't give it to me. I bought it.

FATHER: How could you buy it? You have no money. (*The father seats himself on one of the cushions, left.*)

DAUGHTER: I paid him with two of my pearl haircombs, my writing brush, and the red sash I had at New Year.

FATHER: And that is how Ishimoto grows richer day by day. Sit here opposite me, and let us talk together as we used to when you were a child. *(The daughter seats herself on the cushion opposite him.)* It is here, on this very spot, your old teacher used to teach you your lessons. Don't you remember any longer, with any fondness, all that he told you of our Japanese past, our culture and our wise men, our traditions, and the courageous lives of our history's heroines?

DAUGHTER: I only remember one thing about those lessons, my father.

FATHER: And what is that?

DAUGHTER: That all the two hours my old teacher sat where you sit now and droned into my ear our Japanese past, I was made to sit motionless, so. *(She assumes the rigid posture of the Japanese student.)* Never once was I allowed to move an arm, a hand, or my littlest finger. How the minutes dragged on! I thought he would never finish, that I would turn to stone on the spot and never be able to move again, or run and play in the courtyard.

to drone to speak monotonously

FATHER: It is true the discipline was harsh –

DAUGHTER: One day, I remember, I felt my left foot grow numb and I ventured to move my trunk the tiniest fraction to relieve the pressure on it. My teacher saw me; he gave me a look like the black God of War. Without a word to me, he stopped the lesson; he got up and left without a bow. I could hear him in the next room complaining loudly to you and saying how unworthy I was. I was left crying with fear and shame.

numb frozen stiff, unable to move
trunk main part of the body

FATHER: I remember.

DAUGHTER: From that day on, I had my lessons from him in the outer room with no heat, although it was December and the snow was piled high in the streets. I would turn purple with the cold, but dared not shiver or tremble in the slightest.

FATHER: Yes, yes. Your mother and I discussed it through an entire night.

DAUGHTER: I didn't know you noticed ... or cared.

FATHER: We did. We were afraid it would be too hard on you but we decided, in the dawn light, rightly or wrongly, that discipline was the path to wisdom and virtue. We wanted our daughter to be wise and virtuous. We followed custom.

DAUGHTER: Custom!

FATHER: I know you think custom ancient and barbaric.

DAUGHTER: Yes, I do.

FATHER: Yet it is not. It does not diminish men's actions. It gives those actions form. It is our way of respecting others.

to diminish to make less (important)

DAUGHTER: But it never changes. *(Proudly.)* This is the year 1900, you know.

FATHER: *(Amused.)* A Western year. 1900, eh? Did Mr. Ishimoto give you that information? Perhaps free, with the chair?

DAUGHTER: *(With child-like mysteriousness.)* Oh, I had heard what year it was.

FATHER: Will you believe me if I tell you something?

DAUGHTER: I will try.

FATHER: It is not true that custom fails to change.

DAUGHTER: I don't see that it does.

FATHER: You have not observed it long enough. Do you know

What is the gist of this illustration of the change of times and customs?

loathsome sth you strongly dislike or detest

stubborn extremely inflexible

eavesdropping listening without being noticed

there was a day when meat was never eaten in this house? To eat meat was looked upon as a loathsome evil because the Buddha himself forbade the killing of animals. But gradually the belief began to change. Little by little we were invaded by new ideas from the Western world. I well remember the day I first ordered the preparation of meat in this house. My honoured mother spent that day in her room at her personal shrine praying for all of us who dared to break a tradition over a thousand years old. She ate nothing for three days and for two years and more would not eat with us in this room or go near the kitchen where the meat was prepared. To this very hour she has never tasted it and will not if she lives another hundred years.

DAUGHTER: She is stubborn.

FATHER: We must all be stubborn in what we believe or one day find we believe in nothing.

DAUGHTER: But you said you change your beliefs.

FATHER: I do, and have, and will. When others began to eat meat, I said to myself: Is there some good in this? And I inquired and found there was; that animal flesh makes men stronger and builds muscles to withstand cold and hard work. And so I said, "I will change. We will eat meat in my house." And we did. But not until I had considered it carefully and weighed the custom against the new belief.

DAUGHTER: Perhaps you have changed – in small things.

FATHER: Small things?

DAUGHTER: Eating meat is a small thing to me when I see how chained our lives are.

FATHER: We are not chained. We are civilized and reserved, it is true –

DAUGHTER: You call it civilized and reserved, but I call it a prison. I am in a prison and I yearn to be free. (*Enter mother at centre back. She carries a bowl, crosses to the table and places the bowl on it. She putters about as an excuse for eavesdropping.*)

FATHER: Free to do as you please?

DAUGHTER: Free to do as –

FATHER: As – what?

DAUGHTER: As other women do.

FATHER: What other women?

DAUGHTER: Western women.

FATHER: Ishimoto!

DAUGHTER: Mr. Ishimoto has told me many things; he has painted me a picture of another world – a world I long to know and be a part of. In that world, women are free to grow and blossom instead of sitting with folded hands and allowing life to slip away from them as they do here.

FATHER: Women here live honourable lives.

DAUGHTER: *(Flatly.)* They obey their husbands and bear children and die with never a question on their lips.

FATHER: Is that not honourable?

DAUGHTER: It is not freedom. In the Western lands women do not hide behind shutters and sit in an eternal twilight while others regulate their lives.

FATHER: They do not?

DAUGHTER: No. There they walk freely on the streets or go into teahouses alone and order what they wish and pay for it themselves, for they have their own money.

FATHER: I have heard of that.

DAUGHTER: But, most important, they go to school and learn what men learn. They talk to men as their equals and, Mr. Ishimoto says, a wife may even criticize her husband. *(The mother, who has listened in growing horror, utters an exclamation at this and hurriedly leaves the room.)*

FATHER: My daughter –

DAUGHTER: And it is said that men embrace their wives in front of others and show affection in ways I don't properly understand. But I know it is by more than a bow.

FATHER: It is. I have heard of it. It is called kissing.

DAUGHTER: That's it. That is what Mr. Ishimoto called it.

FATHER: But a kiss is only another custom, strange to us but familiar to them. There is as much feeling of the heart in a bow as there is in a kiss. And yet, to my mind, a bow is in good form because it is an unselfish recognition of another; while a kiss, which is part of love-making, shows a desire for one's own pleasure.

DAUGHTER: It sounds exciting and natural to me.

FATHER: What is natural and what is not? It would seem that all of life must be regulated in some way if we are to live together. One could argue that it is "natural" to have customs to regulate "naturalness."

DAUGHTER: *(Boldly, then hesitatingly.)* I think it is natural for –

FATHER: For what?

DAUGHTER: For a girl to choose her own husband.

FATHER: *(Rises.)* What do you say? Oh, this is too much. I have sat here patiently trying to reason with you, but this is too much.

DAUGHTER: I don't want to marry a man I've never seen.

FATHER: Ungrateful, unfilial child! What do you know, what does any young girl know about choosing a husband? What

➍ What do you think of the role of women in traditional Japanese society?

unfilial not showing respect to one's parents

means *finanzielle Mittel*

can she know of his means, his family, his character, his education, which are what matter in a husband?

DAUGHTER: I *won't!* I *won't* marry him.

FATHER: I draw the line. Finally and firmly. Have all the romantic daydreams you like – no doubt your husband will pay for them – but you *will* marry the man we have chosen for you.

DAUGHTER: (*Beating her hands on the floor.*) No, no, no, no.

FATHER: This is my fault. I should have supervised your education.

DAUGHTER: (*Sobbing.*) Education.

FATHER: But the education of a daughter is always in the hands of the women of the house.

DAUGHTER: (*Triumphantly.*) There, you see? Another *custom!*

Arundhati Roy, The God of Small Things

The novel, published in 1997, tells the story of Rahel and Estha, unidentical twins who are living in the South-Indian state of Kerala in the 1960s. Kerala with its mix of a predominantly Hindu and relatively large Christian and Muslim populations provides an ideal background for the education of the twins, who in their development are exposed to the conflicting forces of their own indigenous culture and its interaction with Western culture and life-style. Just like their parents and their uncles and aunts, they are sent abroad to Europe and the United States to enjoy the privileges of the anglophile Indian upper-middle class. These privileges, however, finally turn out to be a burden as they alienate them from their own immediate environment. The following passage is about the awareness of the repatriates and their "re-dreaming the dream".

ignominy shame

Mammachi had started making pickles commercially soon after Pappachi retired from Government service in Delhi and came to live in Ayemenem. The Kottayam Bible Society was having a fair and asked Mammachi to make some of her famous banana jam and tender mango pickle. It sold quickly, and Mammachi found that she had more orders than she could cope with. Thrilled with her success, she decided to persist with the pickles and jam, and soon found herself busy all year round. Pappachi, for his part, was having trouble coping with the ignominy of retirement. He was seventeen years older than Mammachi, and realized with a shock that he was an old man when his wife was still in her prime.

Though Mammachi had conical corneas and was already practically blind, Pappachi would not help her with the pickle-making, because he did not consider pickle-making a suitable job for a high-ranking ex-Government official. He had always been a jealous man, so he greatly resented the attention his wife was suddenly getting. He slouched around the compound in his immaculately tailored suits, weaving sullen circles around mounds of red chillies and freshly powdered yellow turmeric, watching Mammachi supervise the buying, the weighing, the salting and drying, of limes and tender mangoes. Every night he beat her with a brass flower vase. The beatings weren't new. What was new was only the frequency with which they took place. One night Pappachi broke the bow of Mammachi's violin and threw it in the river.

conical corneas eye disease

What is the relationship between husband and wife like?

Then Chacko came home for a summer vacation from Oxford. He had grown to be a big man, and was, in those days, strong from rowing for Balliol. A week after he arrived he found Pappachi beating Mammachi in the study. Chacko strode into the room, caught Pappachi's vase-hand and twisted it around his back.

Balliol famous Oxford College

'I never want this to happen again,' he told his father. 'Ever.'

For the rest of that day Pappachi sat in the verandah and stared stonily out at the ornamental garden, ignoring the plates of food that Kochu Maria brought him. Late at night he went into his study and brought out his favourite mahogany rocking chair. He put it down in the middle of the driveway and smashed it into little bits with a plumber's monkey wrench. He left it there in the moonlight, a heap of varnished wicker and splintered wood. He never touched Mammachi again. But he never spoke to her either as long as he lived. When he needed anything he used Kochu Maria or Baby Kochamma as intermediaries.

monkey wrench *Schraubenschlüssel*

intermediary *Vermittler*

In the evenings, when he knew visitors were expected, he would sit on the verandah and sew buttons that weren't missing onto his shirts, to create the impression that Mammachi neglected him. To some small degree he did succeed in further corroding Ayemenem's view of working wives.

He bought the skyblue Plymouth from an old Englishman in Munnar. He became a familiar sight in Ayemenem, coasting importantly down the narrow road in his wide car, looking outwardly elegant but sweating freely inside his woollen suits. He wouldn't allow Mammachi or anyone else in the family to use it, or even to sit in it. The Plymouth was Pappachi's revenge.

Why does the narrator refer to Pappachi's car as his "revenge"?

entomologist scientist specialised in the study of insects

dense thick

dorsal tufts hair at the back of the body

taxonomic concerned with the classification of organisms

lepidopterist scientist specialised in the study of butterflies and moths

pernicious malicious, evil

What does the couple's attachment to Europe represent?

Pappachi had been an Imperial Entomologist at the Pusa Institute. After Independence, when the British left, his designation was changed from Imperial Entomologist to Joint Director, Entomology. The year he retired, he had risen to a rank equivalent to Director.

His life's greatest setback was not having had the moth that *he* had discovered named after him.

It fell into his drink one evening while he was sitting on the verandah of a rest house after a long day in the field. As he picked it out he noticed its unusually dense dorsal tufts. He took a closer look. With growing excitement he mounted it, measured it and the next morning placed it in the sun for a few hours for the alcohol to evaporate. Then he caught the first train back to Delhi. To taxonomic attention and, he hoped, fame. After six unbearable months of anxiety, to Pappachi's intense disappointment he was told that his moth had finally been identified as a slightly unusual race of a well-known species that belonged to the tropical family Lymantriidae.

The real blow came twelve years later, when, as a consequence of a radical taxonomic reshuffle, lepidopterists decided that Pappachi's moth *was* in fact a separate species and genus hitherto unknown to science. By then, of course, Pappachi had retired and moved to Ayemenem. It was too late for him to assert his claim to the discovery. His moth was named after the Acting Director of the Department of Entomology, a junior officer whom Pappachi had always disliked.

In the years to come, even though he had been ill-humoured long before he discovered the moth, Pappachi's Moth was held responsible for his black moods and sudden bouts of temper. Its pernicious ghost – grey, furry and with unusually dense dorsal tufts – haunted every house that he ever lived in. It tormented him and his children and his children's children.

Until the day he died, even in the stifling Ayemenem heat, every single day, Pappachi wore a well-pressed three-piece suit and his gold pocket watch. On his dressing table, next to his cologne and silver hairbrush, he kept a picture of himself as a young man, with his hair slicked down, taken in a photographer's studio in Vienna where he had done the six-month diploma course that had qualified him to apply for the post of Imperial Entomologist. It was during those few months they spent in Vienna that Mammachi took her first lessons on the violin. The lessons were abruptly discontinued when Mammachi's teacher, Launsky-Tieffenthal, made the mistake of telling Pappachi that his wife was exceptionally talented and, in his opinion, potentially concert class.

Mammachi pasted, in the family photograph album, the clipping from the *Indian Express* that reported Pappachi's death. It said:

> Noted entomologist, Shri Benaan John Ipe, son of late Rev. E. John Ipe of Ayemenem (popularly known as *Punnyan Kunju),* suffered a massive heart attack and passed away at the Kottayam General Hospital last night. He developed chest pains around 1.05 a.m. and was rushed to hospital. The end came at 2.45 a.m. Shri Ipe had been keeping indifferent health since last six months. He is survived by his wife Soshamma and two children.

At Pappachi's funeral, Mammachi cried and her contact lenses slid around in her eyes. Ammu told the twins that Mammachi was crying more because she was used to him than because she loved him. She was used to having him slouching around the pickle factory, and was used to being beaten from time to time. Ammu said that human beings were creatures of habit, and it was amazing the kind of things they could get used to. You only had to look around you, Ammu said, to see that beatings with brass vases were the least of them.

After the funeral Mammachi asked Rahel to help her to locate and remove her contact lenses with the little orange pipette that came in its own case. Rahel asked Mammachi whether, after Mammachi died, she could inherit the pipette. Ammu took her out of the room and smacked her.

'I never want to hear you discussing people's deaths with them again,' she said.

Estha said Rahel deserved it for being so insensitive.

The photograph of Pappachi in Vienna, with his hair slicked down, was reframed and put up in the drawing room.

He was a photogenic man, dapper and carefully groomed, with a little man's largeish head. He had an incipient second chin that would have been emphasized had he looked down or nodded. In the photograph he had taken care to hold his head high enough to hide his double chin, yet not so high as to appear haughty. His light brown eyes were polite, yet maleficent, as though he was making an effort to be civil to the photographer while plotting to murder his wife. He had a little fleshy knob on the centre of his upper lip that dropped down over his lower lip in a sort of effeminate pout – the kind that children who suck their thumbs develop. He had an elongated dimple on his chin which only served to underline the threat of a lurking manic violence. A sort of contained cruelty. He wore khaki jodhpurs though he had never ridden a horse in his life.

incipient starting to appear

State what image of Pappachi is presented in the photograph. What are the keywords used to characterise him?

haughty arrogant
maleficent wishing evil on others

jodhpurs riding breeches

His riding boots reflected the photographer's studio lights. An ivory-handled riding crop lay neatly across his lap.
There was a watchful stillness to the photograph that lent an underlying chill to the warm room in which it hung.

riding crop whip used to control the horse

When he died, Pappachi left trunks full of expensive suits and a chocolate tin full of cuff-links that Chacko distributed among the taxi drivers in Kottayam. They were separated and made into rings and pendants for unmarried daughters' dowries.
When the twins asked what cuff-links were for – 'To link cuffs together,' Ammu told them – they were thrilled by this morsel of logic in what had so far seemed an illogical language. *Cuff+ link* = *Cuff-link*. This, to them, rivalled the precision and logic of mathematics. *Cuff-links* gave them an inordinate (if exaggerated) satisfaction, and a real affection for the English language.
Ammu said that Pappachi was an incurable British CCP, which was short for *chhi-chhi poach* and in Hindi meant shit-wiper.
Chacko said that the correct word for people like Pappachi was *Anglophile*. He made Rahel and Estha look up *Anglophile* in the *Reader's Digest Great Encyclopaedic Dictionary*. It said *Person well disposed to the English*. Then Estha and Rahel had to look up *disposed*.
It said:

cuff-links *Manschettenknöpfe*

dowry money or gifts brought by a bride to her husband at marriage

Explain the humour of this little anecdote.

(1) Place suitably in particular order.
(2) Bring mind into certain state.
(3) Do what one will with, get off one's hands, stow away, demolish, finish, settle, consume (food), kill, sell.

Chacko said that in Pappachi's case it meant (2) *Bring mind into certain state*. Which, Chacko said, meant that Pappachi's mind had been *brought into a state* which made him like the English.
Chacko told the twins that though he hated to admit it, they were all Anglophiles. They were *a family* of Anglophiles. Pointed in the wrong direction, trapped outside their own history, and unable to retrace their steps because their footprints had been swept away. He explained to them that history was like an old house at night. With all the lamps lit. And ancestors whispering inside.
'To understand history,' Chacko said, 'we have to go inside and listen to what they're saying. And look at the books and the pictures on the wall. And smell the smells.'
Estha and Rahel had no doubt that the house Chacko meant was the house on the other side of the river, in the middle of the abandoned rubber estate where they had never been. Kari

Interpret the following extended metaphor in the light of intercultural relationships.

Saipu's house. The Black Sahib. The Englishman who had 'gone native'. Who spoke Malayalam and wore mundus. Ayemenem's own Kurtz. Ayemenem his private Heart of Darkness. He had shot himself through the head ten years ago when his young lover's parents had taken the boy away from him and sent him to school. After the suicide, the property had become the subject of extensive litigation between Kari Saipu's cook and his secretary. The house had lain empty for years. Very few people had seen it. But the twins could picture it.

The History House.

With cool stone floors and dim walls and billowing ship-shaped shadows. Plump, translucent lizards lived behind old pictures, and waxy, crumbling ancestors with tough toe-nails and breath that smelled of yellow maps gossiped in sibilant, papery whispers.

'But we can't go in,' Chacko explained, 'because we've been locked out. And when we look in through the windows, all we see are shadows. And when we try and listen, all we hear is a whispering. And we cannot understand the whispering, because our minds have been invaded by a war. A war that we have won and lost. The very worst sort of war. A war that captures dreams and re-dreams them. A war that has made us adore our conquerors and despise ourselves.'

➜ What does this reversed image imply?

mundus special Indian dress
Kurtz reference to T. S. Eliot's poem "The Hollow Men" (1925)
Heart of Darkness novel by Joseph Conrad (1857–1924)
litigation lawsuit

➜ Outline what Chacko refers to with the image of that war?

Multi-ethnicity: World-wide terrorism

Julian Barnes, The Visitors

This is one complete chapter of the author's novel *A History of the World in 10½ Chapters.* It is about terrorism and describes the scenario of a ship hijacking, which comes close to real hijackings. This is set against the frame of a combined educational and pleasure cruise and the self reflections of Franklin Hughes who starts as both a fun-seeking participant and a rather devoted lecturer on the history of culture in general and the history of the civilisations of the Mediterranean and the Middle East in particular, but ends, above all, as a disillusioned commentator on the inevitable consequences. His role as negotiator and mediator

almost makes him an accomplice in the selection of the potential victims and their subsequent killing. Accordingly, what begins as a humorous, sometimes satirical classification of the members of different nations and cultures finally results in another deadly episode in the blood-stained history of the Middle East.
The author makes ample use of clichés and of the sometimes absurdly superficial classification and division of people according to nationality.

bonhomie (Fr.) good humour, friendliness

Why does the author use stereotypes to characterise the different nationalities of the cruise passengers?

decorous showing good taste

hue shade, tone

paunch belly

sturdy-kneed having large, strong knees

rangy long, slender

complexion colour of the skin

ostentatious clearly visible

Franklin Hughes had come on board an hour earlier to extend some necessary bonhomie towards those who would make his job easier over the next twenty days. Now, he leaned on the rail and watched the passengers climb the gangway: middle-aged and elderly couples for the most part, some bearing an obvious stamp of nationality, others, more decorous, preserving for the moment a sly anonymity of origin. Franklin, his arm lightly but unarguably around the shoulder of his travelling companion, played his annual game of guessing where his audience came from. Americans were the easiest, the men in New World leisure-wear of pastel hues, the women unconcerned by throbbing paunches. The British were the next easiest, the men in Old World tweed jackets hiding short-sleeved shirts of ochre or beige, the women sturdy-kneed and keen to tramp any mountain at the sniff of a Greek temple. There were two Canadian couples whose towelling hats bore a prominent maple-leaf emblem; a rangy Swedish family with four heads of blond hair; some confusable French and Italians whom Franklin identified with a simple mutter of *baguette* or *macaroni;* and six Japanese who declined their stereotype by not displaying a single camera among them. With the exception of a few family groups and the occasional lone aesthetic-looking Englishman, they came up the gangway in obedient couples.
'The animals came in two by two,' Franklin commented. He was a tall, fleshy man somewhere in his forties, with pale gold hair and a reddish complexion which the envious put down to drink and the charitable to an excess of sun; his face seemed familiar in a way which made you forget to ask whether or not you judged it good-looking. His companion, or assistant, but not, she would insist, secretary, was a slim, dark girl displaying clothes newly bought for the cruise. Franklin, ostentatiously an old hand, wore a khaki bush-shirt and a pair of rumpled jeans. While it was not quite the uniform some of the passengers expected of a distinguished guest lecturer, it accurately suggested the origin of such distinction as Franklin could command. If he'd been an American academic he might

have dug out a seersucker suit; if a British academic, perhaps a creased linen jacket the colour of ice-cream. But Franklin's fame (which was not quite as extensive as he thought it) came from television. He had started as a mouthpiece for other people's views, a young man in a corduroy suit with an affable and unthreatening way of explaining culture. After a while he realized that if he could speak this stuff there was no reason why he shouldn't write it as well. At first it was no more than 'additional material by Franklin Hughes', then a co-script credit, and finally the achievement of a full 'written and presented by Franklin Hughes' . What his special area of knowledge was nobody could quite discern, but he roved freely in the worlds of archaeology, history and comparative culture. He specialized in the contemporary allusion which would rescue and enliven for the average viewer such dead subjects as Hannibal's crossing of the Alps, or Viking treasure hoards in East Anglia, or Herod's palaces. 'Hannibal's elephants were the panzer divisions of their age,' he would declare as he passionately straddled a foreign landscape; or, 'That's as many foot-soldiers as could be fitted into Wembley Stadium on Cup Final Day'; or, 'Herod wasn't just a tyrant and a unifier of his country, he was also a patron of the arts – perhaps we should think of him as a sort of Mussolini with good taste.'

Franklin's television fame soon brought him a second wife, and a couple of years later a second divorce. Nowadays, his contracts with Aphrodite Cultural Tours always included the provision of a cabin for his assistant; the crew of the *Santa Euphemia* noted with admiration that the assistants tended not to last from one voyage to the next. Franklin was generous towards the stewards, and popular with those who had paid a couple of thousand pounds for their twenty days. He had the engaging habit of sometimes pursuing a favourite digression so fervently that he would have to stop and look around with a puzzled smile before reminding himself where he was meant to be. Many of the passengers commented to one another on Franklin's obvious enthusiasm for his subject, how refreshing it was in these cynical times, and how he really made history come alive for them. If his bush-shirt was often carelessly buttoned and his denim trousers occasionally stained with lobster, this was no more than corroboration of his beguiling zeal for the job. His clothes hinted, too, at the admirable democracy of learning in the modern age: you evidently did not have to be a stuffy professor in a wing-collar to understand the principles of Greek architecture.

'The Welcome Buffet's at eight,' said Franklin. 'Think I'd better

seersucker suit light linen suit with wrinkled surface

corduroy *Cord*

affable showing friendlines

to discern to recognise clearly

➊ What is so special about Franklin's technique of "contemporary allusion"?

to straddle to walk with one's legs far apart

engaging charming

digression *Ablenkung*

corroboration confirmation

beguiling fascinating

zeal enthusiasm

stuffy boring

wing-collar stiff shirt collar

spiel (orig. Germ., Am. sl.) clever talk designed to impress or persuade
Tricia short for Patricia
to go stale to lose interest or flavour
to recede to become smaller
to flake to peel
researcher sb investigating a problem
superstitious *abergläubisch*
nominal small, unimportant
fake not real, not authentic

A popular criticism of television and the media people. Think of a possible function of this motif in the text.

to sneer to show contempt

put in a couple of hours on my spiel for tomorrow morning.'
'Surely you've done that lots of times before?' Tricia was half-hoping he would stay on deck with her as they sailed out into the Gulf of Venice.
'Got to make it different each year. Otherwise you go stale.' He touched her lightly on the forearm and went below. In fact, his opening address at ten the next morning would be exactly the same as for the previous five years. The only difference – the only thing designed to prevent Franklin from going stale – was the presence of Tricia instead of ... of, what was that last girl's name? But he liked to maintain the fiction of working on his lectures beforehand, and he could easily pass up the chance of seeing Venice recede yet again. It would still be there the following year, a centimetre or two nearer the waterline, its pinky complexion, like his own, flaking a little more.
On deck, Tricia gazed at the city until the campanile of San Marco became a pencil-stub. She had first met Franklin three months ago, when he'd appeared on the chat-show for which she was a junior researcher. They'd been to bed a few times, but not much so far. She had told the girls at the flat she was going away with a schoolfriend; if things went well, she'd let on when she got back, but for the moment she was a little superstitious. Franklin Hughes! And he'd been really considerate so far, even allotting her some nominal duties so that she wouldn't look too much like just a girlfriend. So many people in television struck her as a bit fake – charming, yet not altogether honest. Franklin was just the same offscreen as on: outgoing, jokey, eager to tell you things. You believed what he said. Television critics made fun of his clothes and the tuft of chest-hair where his shirt parted, and sometimes they sneered at what he said, but that was just envy, and she'd like to see some of those critics get up and try to perform like Franklin. Making it look easy, he had explained to her at their first lunch, was the hardest thing of all. The other secret about television, he said, was how to know when to shut up and let the pictures do the work for you – 'You've got to get that fine balance between word and image.' Privately, Franklin was hoping for the ultimate credit: 'Written, narrated and produced by Franklin Hughes'. In his dreams he sometimes choreographed for himself a gigantic walking shot in the Forum which would take him from the Arch of Septimius Severus to the Temple of Vesta. Where to put the camera was the only problem.
The first leg of the trip, as they steamed down the Adriatic,

went much as usual. There was the Welcome Buffet, with the crew sizing up the passengers and the passengers warily circling one another; Franklin's opening lecture, in which he flattered his audience, deprecated his television fame and announced that it was a refreshing change to be addressing real people instead of a glass eye and a cameraman shouting 'Hair in the gate, can we do it again, love?' (the technical reference would be lost on most of his listeners, which was intended by Franklin: they were allowed to be snobbish about TV, but not to assume it was idiots' business); and then there was Franklin's other opening lecture, one just as necessary to bring off, in which he explained to his assistant how the main thing they must remember was to have a good time. Sure he'd have to work – indeed, there'd be times when much as he didn't want to he'd be forced to shut himself away in his cabin with his notes – but mostly he felt they should treat it as three weeks' holiday from the filthy English weather and all that backstabbing at Television Centre. Tricia nodded agreement, though as a junior researcher she had not yet witnessed, let alone endured, any backstabbing. A more worldly-wise girl would have readily understood Franklin to mean 'Don't expect anything more out of me than this'. Tricia, being placid and optimistic, glossed his little speech more mildly as 'Let's be careful of building up false expectations' – which to do him credit was roughly what Franklin Hughes intended. He fell lightly in love several times each year, a tendency in himself which he would occasionally deplore but regularly indulge. However, he was far from heartless, and the moment he felt a girl – especially a nice girl – needing him more than he needed her a terrible flush of apprehension would break out in him. This rustling panic would usually make him suggest one of two things – either that the girl move into his flat, or that she move out of his life – neither of which he exactly wanted. So his address of welcome to Jenny or Cathy or in this case Tricia came more from prudence than cynicism, though when things subsequently went awry it was unsurprising if Jenny or Cathy or in this case Tricia remembered him as more calculating than in fact he had been.

The same prudence, murmuring insistently at him across numerous gory news reports, had made Franklin Hughes acquire an Irish passport. The world was no longer a welcoming place where the old dark-blue British job, topped up with the words 'journalist' and 'BBC', got you what you wanted. 'Her Britannic Majesty's Secretary of State,' Franklin could quote from memory, 'Requests and requires in the Name of

wary cautious

to deprecate to minimize or belittle

backstabbing (fig.) saying bad things about people behind their backs

placid calm, peaceful

to deplore to express/feel sadness about
deploring, deplorable, deplorableness

to indulge to to enjoy to excess

prudence caution

awry off course

gory bloodthirsty

job here: example of an object, in this case the passport

Her Majesty all those whom it may concern to allow the bearer such assistance and protection as may be necessary.' Wishful thinking. Nowadays Franklin travelled on a green Irish passport with a gold harp on the cover, which made him feel like a Guinness rep every time he produced it. Inside, the word 'journalist' was also missing from Hughes's largely honest self-description. There were countries in the world which didn't welcome journalists, and who thought that white-skinned ones pretending interest in archaeological sites were obviously British spies. The less compromising 'Writer' was also intended as a piece of self-encouragement. If Franklin described himself as a writer, then this might nudge him into becoming one. Next time round, there was a definite chance for a book-of-the-series; and beyond that he was toying with something serious but sexy – like a personal history of the world – which might roost for months in the bestseller lists.

The *Santa Euphemia* was an elderly but comfortable ship with a courtly Italian captain and an efficient Greek crew. These Aphrodite Tours brought a predictable clientèle, disparate in nationality but homogeneous in taste. The sort of people who preferred reading to deck quoits, and sun-bathing to the disco. They followed the guest lecturer everywhere, took most of the supplementary trips and disdained straw donkeys in the souvenir shops. They had not come for romance, though a string trio occasionally incited some old-fashioned dancing. They took their turn at the captain's table, were inventive when it came to fancy-dress night, and dutifully read the ship's newspaper, which printed their daily route alongside birthday messages and non-controversial events happening on the European continent.

The atmosphere seemed a little torpid to Tricia, but it was a well-organized torpor. As in the address to his assistant, Franklin had emphasized in his opening lecture that the purpose of the next three weeks was pleasure and relaxation. He hinted tactfully that people had different levels of interest in classical antiquity, and that he for one wouldn't be keeping an attendance book and marking down absentees with a black X. Franklin engagingly admitted that there were occasions when even he could tire of yet another row of Corinthian columns standing against a cloudless sky; though he did this in a way which allowed the passengers to disbelieve him.

The tail end of the Northern winter had been left behind; and at a stately pace the *Santa Euphemia* took its contented passengers into a calm Mediterranean spring. Tweed jackets gave way

rep short for (sales) representative

compromising exposing to danger

to nudge to push gently

to roost to rest, to stay

Santa Euphemia ship's (telling) name

courtly polite

disparate very different

homogeneous alike
homogeneity (opposite of **heterogeneity**)

quoits game in which rings are thrown onto small poles

disdain to show contempt for

inventive creative, skilled
to invent, invention

torpid lethargic

torpor inactivity

to linen ones, trouser-suits to slightly outdated sun-dresses. They passed through the Corinth Canal at night, with some of the passengers jammed against a porthole in their night-clothes, and the hardier ones on deck, occasionally letting off ineffectual bursts of flash from their cameras. From the Ionian to the Aegean: it was a little fresher and choppier in the Cyclades, but nobody minded. They went ashore at chichi Mykonos, where an elderly headmaster twisted his ankle while climbing among the ruins; at marbled Paros and volcanic Thira. The cruise was ten days old when they stopped at Rhodes. While the passengers were ashore the *Santa Euphemia* took on fuel, vegetables, meat and more wine. It also took on some visitors, although this did not become apparent until the following morning.

They were steaming towards Crete, and at eleven o'clock Franklin began his usual lecture on Knossos and Minoan Civilization. He had to be a little careful, because his audience tended to know about Knossos, and some of them would have their personal theories. Franklin liked people asking questions; he didn't mind pieces of obscure and even correct information being added to what he had already imparted – he would offer thanks with a courtly bow and a murmur of 'Herr Professor', implying that as long as some of us have an overall grasp of things, it was fine for others to fill their heads with recondite detail; but what Franklin Hughes couldn't stand were bores with pet ideas they couldn't wait to try out on the guest lecturer. Excuse me, Mr Hughes, it looks very Egyptian to me – how do we know the Egyptians didn't build it? Aren't you assuming that Homer wrote when people think he (a little laugh) – or she – did? I don't have any actual expert knowledge, yet surely it would make more sense if ... There was always at least one of them, playing the puzzled yet reasonable amateur; unfooled by received opinion, he – or she – knew that historians were full of bluff, and that complicated matters were best understood using zestful intuition untainted by any actual knowledge or research. 'I appreciate what you're saying, Mr Hughes, but surely it would be more logical ... ' What Franklin occasionally wanted to say, though never did, was that these brisk guesses about earlier civilizations seemed to him to have their foundation as often as not in Hollywood epics starring Kirk Douglas or Burt Lancaster. He imagined himself hearing out one of these jokers and replying, with a skirl of irony on the adverb, 'Of course, you realize that the film of Ben Hur isn't *entirely* reliable?' But not this trip. In fact, not until he knew it was going to be his last trip. Then he

porthole round window on a ship

chichi snobbish, high-class

Can you explain Franklin's reactions to and comments on communicative strategies and interaction?

recondite abstruse

bore boring person

pet here: favourite

received here: accepted

zestful keen, full of energy

untainted not influenced

skirl shrill tone

could let go a little. He could be franker with his audience, less careful with the booze, more receptive to the flirting glance.

The visitors were late for Franklin Hughes's lecture on Knossos, and he had already done the bit in which he pretended to be Sir Arthur Evans when they opened the double doors and fired a single shot into the ceiling. Franklin, still headily involved in his own performance, murmured, 'Can I have a translation of that?' but it was an old joke, and not enough to recapture the passengers' attention. They had already forgotten Knossos and were watching the tall man with a moustache and glasses who was coming to take Franklin's place at the lectern. Under normal circumstances, Franklin might have yielded him the microphone after a courteous inquiry about his credentials. But given that the man was carrying a large machine-gun and wore one of those red check headdresses which used to be shorthand for lovable desert warriors loyal to Lawrence of Arabia but in recent years had become shorthand for baying terrorists eager to massacre the innocent, Franklin simply made a vague 'Over to you' gesture with his hands and sat down on his chair.

Franklin's audience – as he still thought of them in a brief proprietorial flurry – fell silent. Everyone was avoiding an incautious movement; each breath was discreetly taken. There were three visitors, and the other two were guarding the double doors into the lecture room. The tall one with the glasses had an almost scholarly air as he tapped the microphone in the manner of lecturers everywhere: partly to see if it was working, partly to attract attention. The second half of this gesture was not strictly necessary.

'I apologize for the inconvenience,' he began, setting off a nervous laugh or two. 'But I am afraid it is necessary to interrupt your holiday for a while. I hope it will not be a long interruption. You will all stay here, sitting exactly where you are, until we tell you what to do.'

A voice, male, angry and American, asked from the middle of the auditorium, 'Who are you and what the hell do you want?' The Arab swayed back to the microphone he had just left, and with the contemptuous suavity of a diplomat, replied, 'I am sorry, I am not taking questions at this juncture.' Then, just to make sure he was not mistaken for a diplomat, he went on. 'We are not people who believe in unnecessary violence. However, when I fired the shot into the ceiling to attract your attention, I had set this little catch here so that the gun only fires one shot at a time. If I change the catch' – he did so while

booze (ifml) alcohol

moustache *Schnurrbart*

lectern reading stand for a speaker

to yield to let sb have sth

credential proof of quality and authority
creed, credible, credit, to credit, creditable

baying shouting

proprietorial showing ownership

flurry sudden motion or feeling

inconvenience trouble, unpleasantness

contemptuous showing a lack of respect
contempt, contemptible, contemptibleness

suavity smoothness

juncture critical moment

catch *Sicherung*

holding the weapon half-aloft like an arms instructor with an exceptionally ignorant class – 'the gun will continue to fire until the magazine is empty. I hope that is clear.'

aloft in the air

The Arab left the hall. People held hands; there were occasional sniffs and sobs, but mostly silence. Franklin glanced across to the far left of the auditorium at Tricia. His assistants were allowed to come to his lectures, though not to sit in direct line of sight – 'Mustn't start me thinking about the wrong thing.' She didn't appear frightened, more apprehensive about what the form was. Franklin wanted to say, 'Look, this hasn't happened to me before, it isn't normal, I don't know what to do,' but settled instead for an indeterminate nod. After ten minutes of stiff-necked silence, an American woman in her mid-fifties stood up. Immediately one of the two visitors guarding the door shouted at her. She took no notice, just as she ignored the whispers and grabbing hand of her husband. She walked down the central aisle to the gunmen, stopped a couple of yards short and said in a clear, slow voice suppurating with panic, 'I have to go to the goddam bathroom.'

Check all the references to "the Arab(s)" and state what they have in common.

indeterminate uncertain, not definite

to suppurate to be full of, flow over with

The Arabs neither replied nor looked her in the eye. Instead, with a small gesture of their guns, they indicated as surely as such things can be that she was currently a large target and that any further advance would confirm the fact in an obvious and final way. She turned, walked back to her seat and began to cry. Another woman on the right of the hall immediately started sobbing. Franklin looked across at Tricia again, nodded, got to his feet, deliberately didn't look at the two guards, and went across to the lectern. 'As I was saying ...' He gave an authoritative cough and all eyes reverted to him. 'I was saying that the Palace of Knossos was not by any means the first human settlement on the site. What we think of as the Minoan strata reach down to about seventeen feet, but below this there are signs of human habitation down to twenty-six feet or so. There was life where the palace was built for at least ten thousand years before the first stone was laid ...'

to revert to go back to

It seemed normal to be lecturing again. It also felt as if some feathered cloak of leadership had been thrown over him. He decided to acknowledge this, glancingly at first. Did the guards understand English? Perhaps. Had they ever been to Knossos? Unlikely. So Franklin, while describing the council chamber at the palace, invented a large clay tablet which, he claimed, had probably hung over the gypsum throne. It read – he looked towards the Arabs at this point – 'We are living in difficult times'. As he continued describing the site, he

Looking for a strategy for survival.

gypsum white or colourless mineral used for cement or plaster

scabbard holder for sword or dagger

to latch on to understand

to assent to agree

stiff upper lip (fig.) self-restraint in showing emotion usually associated with the British

aphorism short saying expressing a general truth

conciliatory trying to be friendly

heedful keeping in mind

delay cause of lateness

unearthed more tablets, many of which, as he now fearlessly began to point out, had a universal message. 'We must above all not do anything rash', one said. Another: 'Empty threats are as useless as empty scabbards'. Another: 'The tiger always waits before it springs' (Hughes wondered briefly if Minoan Civilization knew about tigers). He was not sure how many of his audience had latched on to what he was doing, but there came an occasional assenting growl. In a curious way, he was also enjoying himself. He ended his tour of the palace with one of the least typically Minoan of his many inscriptions: 'There is a great power where the sun sets which will not permit certain things'. Then he shuffled his notes together and sat down to warmer applause than usual. He looked across at Tricia and winked. She had tears in her eyes. He glanced towards the two Arabs and thought, that's shown you, now you can see what we're made of, there's some stiff upper lip for you. He rather wished he'd made up some Minoan aphorism about people who wore red tea-towels on their heads, but recognized he wouldn't have had the nerve. He'd keep that one for later, after they were all safe.

They waited for half an hour in a silence that smelt of urine before the leader of the visitors returned. He had a brief word with the guards and walked up the aisle to the lectern. 'I understand that you have been lectured on the palace of Knossos,' he began, and Franklin felt sweat burst into the palms of his hands. 'That is good. It is important for you to understand other civilizations. How they are great, and how' – he paused meaningfully – 'they fall. I hope very much that you will enjoy your trip to Knossos.'

He was leaving the microphone when the same American voice, this time more conciliatory in tone, as if heedful of the Minoan tablets, said, 'Excuse me, would you be able to tell us roughly who you are and roughly what you want?'

The Arab smiled. 'I am not sure that would be a good idea at this stage.' He gave a nod to indicate he had finished, then paused, as if a civil question at least deserved a civil answer. 'Let me put it this way. If things go according to plan, you will soon be able to continue your explorations of the Minoan Civilization. We shall disappear just as we came, and we shall seem to you simply to have been a dream. Then you can forget us. You will remember only that we were a small delay. So there is no need for you to know who we are or where we come from or what we want.'

He was about to leave the low podium when Franklin, rather to his own surprise, said, 'Excuse me.' The Arab turned. 'No more questions.' Hughes went on, 'This is not a question. I just think ... I'm sure you've got other things on your mind ... if we're going to have to stay here you ought to let us go to the lavatory.' The leader of the visitors frowned. 'The bathroom,' Franklin explained; then again, 'the toilet.'

'Of course. You will be able to go to the toilet when we move you.'

'When will that be?' Franklin felt himself a little carried away by his self-appointed role. For his part the Arab noted some unacceptable lack of compliance. He replied brusquely, 'When we decide.'

compliance giving in to others, cooperation

He left. Ten minutes later an Arab they had not seen before came in and whispered to Hughes. He stood up. 'They are going to move us from here to the dining-room. We are to be moved in twos. Occupants of the same cabin are to identify themselves as such. We will be taken to our cabins, where we will be allowed to go to the lavatory. We are also to collect our passports, but nothing else.' The Arab whispered again. 'And we are not allowed to lock the lavatory door.' Without being asked, Franklin went on, 'I think these visitors to the ship are quite serious. I don't think we should do anything which might upset them.'

➔ Why the passports? Explain.

Only one guard was available to move the passengers, and the process took several hours. As Franklin and Tricia were being taken to C deck, he remarked to her, in the casual tone of one commenting on the weather, 'Take the ring off your right hand and put it on your wedding finger. Turn the stone round so that you can't see it. Don't do it now, do it when you're having a pee.'

When they reached the dining-room their passports were examined by a fifth Arab. Tricia was sent to the far end, where the British had been put in one corner and the Americans in another. In the middle of the room were the French, the Italians, two Spaniards and the Canadians. Nearest the door were the Japanese, the Swedes and Franklin, the solitary Irishman. One of the last couples to be brought in were the Zimmermanns, a pair of stout, well-dressed Americans. Hughes had at first placed the husband in the garment business, some master cutter who had set up on his own; but a conversation on Paros had revealed him to be a recently retired professor of philosophy from the Midwest. As the couple passed Franklin's table on their way to the American quarter, Zimmermann muttered lightly, 'Separating the clean from the unclean.'

➔ The implications of Zimmermann's statement?

When they were all present, Franklin was taken off to the purser's office, where the leader was installed. He found himself wondering if the slightly bulbous nose and the moustache

purser officer responsible for the passengers on a ship or plane

bulbous large and rounded

were by any chance attached to the glasses; perhaps they all came off together.

'Ah, Mr Hughes. You seem to be their spokesman. At any event, now your position is official. You will explain to them the following. We are doing our best to make them comfortable, but they must realize that there are certain difficulties. They will be allowed to talk to one another for five minutes at each hour. At the same time those who wish to go to the toilet will be allowed to do so. One person at a time. I can see that they are all sensible people and would not like them to decide not to be sensible. There is one man who says he cannot find his passport. He says he is called Talbot.'

sensible reasonable, having good sense
sensibility, to sense, sensitive, sensitivity

'Mr Talbot, yes.' A vague, elderly Englishman who tended to ask questions about religion in the Ancient World. A mild fellow with no theories of his own, thank God.

'He is to sit with the Americans.'

'But he's British. He comes from Kidderminster.'

'If he remembers where his passport is and he is British he can sit with the British.'

'You can tell he's British. I can vouch for him being British.'

to vouch for to personally guarantee

The Arab looked unimpressed. 'He doesn't talk like an American, does he?'

'I have not talked to him. Still, talking is not proof, is it? You, I think, talk like a British but your passport says you are not a British.' Franklin nodded slowly. 'So we will wait for the passport.'

'Why are you separating us like this?'

'We think you will like to sit with one another.' The Arab made a sign for him to go.

'There's one other thing. My wife. Can she sit with me?'

'Your wife?' The man looked at a list of passengers in front of him. 'You have no wife.'

'Yes I do. She's travelling as Tricia Maitland. It's her maiden name. We were married three weeks ago.' Franklin paused, then added in a confessional tone, 'My third wife, actually.'

But the Arab seemed unimpressed by Franklin's harem. 'You were married three weeks ago? And yet it seems you do not share the same cabin. Are things going so badly?'

'No, I have a separate cabin for my work, you see. The lecturing. It's a luxury, having another cabin, a privilege.'

'She is your wife?' The tone gave nothing away.

'Yes she is,' he replied, mildly indignant.

indignant feeling anger
dignity, to dignify

'But she has a British passport.'

'She's Irish. You become Irish if you marry an Irishman. It's Irish law.'

'Mr Hughes, she has a British passport.' He shrugged as if the dilemma were insoluble, then found a solution. 'But if you wish to sit with your wife, then you may go and sit with her at the British table.'

Franklin smiled awkwardly. 'If I'm the passengers' spokesman, how do I get to see you to pass on the passengers' demands?'

'The passengers' demands? No, you have not understood. The passengers do not have demands. You do not see me unless I want to see you.'

After Franklin had relayed the new orders, he sat at his table by himself and thought about the position. The good part was that so far they had been treated with reasonable civility; no-one had yet been beaten up or shot, and their captors didn't seem to be the hysterical butchers they might have expected. On the other hand, the bad part lay quite close to the good part: being unhysterical, the visitors might also prove reliable, efficient, hard to divert from their purpose. And what was their purpose? Why had they hijacked the *Santa Euphemia?* Who were they negotiating with? And who was steering the sodding ship, which as far as Franklin could tell was going round in large, slow circles?

From time to time, he would nod encouragingly to the Japanese at the next table. Passengers at the far end of the dining-room, he couldn't help noting, would occasionally look up in his direction, as if checking that he was still there. He'd become the liaison man, perhaps even the leader. That Knossos lecture, in the circumstances, had been little short of brilliant; a lot more ballsy than he'd imagined possible. It was the sitting alone like this that got him down; it made him brood. His initial burst of emotion – something close to exhilaration – was seeping away; in its place came lethargy and apprehension. Perhaps he should go and sit with Tricia and the Brits. But then they might take his citizenship away from him. This dividing-up of the passengers: did it mean what he feared it might mean?

Late that afternoon they heard a plane fly over, quite low. There was a muted cheer from the American section of the dining-room; then the plane went away. At six o'clock one of the Greek stewards appeared with a large tray of sandwiches; Franklin noted the effect of fear on hunger. At seven, as he went for a pee, an American voice whispered, 'Keep up the good work.' Back at his table, he tried to look soberly confident. The trouble was, the more he reflected, the less cheerful he felt. In recent years Western governments had

captor sb taking hostages

to divert to turn away from

to negotiate *verhandeln*
negotiable, negotiator, negotiation

sodding (ifml) expression added to show anger

liaison contact, go-between

ballsy (taboo) showing bravery

to brood here: to think deeply
exhilaration cheerfulness

been noisy about terrorism, about standing tall and facing down the threat; but the threat never seemed to understand that it was being faced down, and continued much as before. Those in the middle got killed; governments and terrorists survived.

At nine Franklin was summoned again to the purser's office. The passengers were to be moved for the night: the Americans back to the lecture hall, the British to the disco, and so on. These separate encampments would then be locked. It was necessary: the visitors had to get their sleep as well. Passports were to be held ready for inspection at all times.

'What about Mr Talbot?'

'He has become an honorary American. Until he finds his passport.'

'What about my wife?'

'Miss Maitland. What about her?'

'Can she join me?'

'Ah. Your British wife.'

'She's Irish. You marry an Irishman you become Irish. It's the law.'

'The law, Mr Hughes. People are always telling *us* what is the law. I am often puzzled by what they consider is lawful and what is unlawful.' He looked away to a map of the Mediterranean on the wall behind Franklin. 'Is it lawful to drop bombs on refugee camps, for instance? I have often tried to discover the law which says this is permissible. But it is a long argument, and sometimes I think argument is pointless, just as the law is pointless.' He gave a dismissive shrug. 'As for the matter of Miss Maitland, let us hope that her nationality does not become, how shall I put it, relevant.'

Franklin tried to damp down a shudder. There were times when euphemism could be much more frightening than direct threat. 'Are you able to tell me when it might become ... relevant?'

'They are stupid, you see. They are stupid because they think we are stupid. They lie in the most obvious way. They say they do not have the authority to act. They say arrangements cannot be made quickly. Of course they can. There is such a thing as the telephone. If they think they have learned something from previous incidents of this kind, they are stupid not to realize that we have too. We know about their tactics, the lying and the delays, all this establishing of some kind of relationship with the freedom fighters. We know all that. And we know about the limits of the body for taking action. So we are obliged by your governments to do what we say we will

refugee sb driven out of the home country

permissible allowed
to permit, permission, permissive, permissiveness

dismissive showing indifference, lack of interest

euphemism polite word used instead of sth offensive

previous occurring before sth else in time
incident significant event

do. If they started negotiating at once, there would be no problem. But they only start when it is too late. It is on their heads.'

'No,' said Franklin. 'It's on our heads.'

'You, Mr Hughes, I think, do not have to worry so soon.'

'How soon is soon?'

'Indeed, I think you may not have to worry at all.'

'How soon is soon?'

The leader paused, then made a regretful gesture. 'Tomorrow some time. The timetable, you see, is fixed. We have told them from the beginning.'

Part of Franklin Hughes could not believe he was having this conversation. Another part wanted to say he had always supported the cause of his captors – whatever that cause might be – and incidentally the Gaelic on his passport meant that he was a member of the IRA, and for Christ's sake could he please go to his cabin and lie down and forget all about it. Instead, he repeated, 'Timetable?' The Arab nodded. Without thinking, Franklin said, 'One an hour?' Immediately, he wished he hadn't asked. For all he knew he was giving the fellow ideas.

IRA Irish Republican Army, organisation held partly responsible for terrorism in Northern Ireland.

The Arab shook his head. 'Two. A pair every hour. Unless you raise the stakes they do not take you seriously.'

to raise the stakes to increase one's commitment

'Christ. Just coming on board and killing people just like that. Just like that?'

'You think it would be better if we explained to them why we were killing them?' The tone was sarcastic.

'Well, yes, actually.'

'Do you think they would be sympathetic?' Now there was more mockery than sarcasm. Franklin was silent. He wondered when the killing was due to start. 'Goodnight, Mr Hughes,' said the leader of the visitors.

Franklin was put for the night in a stateroom with the Swedish family and the three Japanese couples. They were, he deduced, the safest group among the passengers. The Swedes because their nation was famously neutral; Franklin and the Japanese presumably because in recent times Ireland and Japan had produced terrorists. How ludicrous. The six Japanese who had come on a cultural cruise in Europe hadn't been asked whether they supported the various political killers in their own country; nor had Franklin been quizzed about the IRA. A Guinness passport awarded through some genealogical fluke suggested the possibility of sympathy with the visitors, and this was his protection. In fact, Franklin hated the IRA, just as he hated any political group which interfered, or might

to deduce to find an answer by using logic

fluke unexpected good luck

homicidal related to murder
maniac crazy person

burdened weighed down with sth

complicity involvement in a crime

A variation of the theme of "Them" versus "Us".

The logic of terrorism.

interfere, with the fulltime job of being Franklin Hughes. For all he knew – and in accordance with his annual policy he had not asked – Tricia was far more sympathetic to the various worldwide groups of homicidal maniacs indirectly committed to interrupting the career of Franklin Hughes. Yet she was herded in with the diabolic British.

There was little talk in the stateroom that night. The Japanese kept to themselves; the Swedish family spent the time trying to distract their children by talking of home and Christmas and British football teams; while Franklin felt burdened by what he knew. He was scared and sickened; but isolation seemed to breed complicity with his captors. He tried thinking of his two wives and the daughter who must be – what? – fifteen now: he always had to remember the year of her birth and work it out from there. He should get down to see her more often. Perhaps he could take her with him when they filmed the next series. She could watch his famous walking shot in the Forum; she'd like that. Now where could he place the camera? Or perhaps a tracking shot. And some extras in toga and sandals – yes, he liked it ...

Next morning Franklin was taken to the purser's office. The leader of the visitors waved him to sit down. 'I have decided to take your advice.'

'My advice?'

'The negotiations, I fear, are going badly. That is to say, there are no negotiations. We have explained our position but they are extremely unwilling to explain their position.'

'They?'

'They. So, unless things change very quickly, we shall be forced to put some pressure on them.'

'Pressure?' Even Franklin, who could not have made a career in television without skill in trading euphemisms, was enraged. 'You mean killing people.'

'That is the only pressure, sadly, which they understand.'

'What about trying other sorts?'

'But we have. We have tried sitting on our hands and waiting for world opinion to come to our help. We have tried being good and hoping that we would be rewarded by getting our land back. I can assure you that these systems do not work.'

'Why not try something in between?'

'An embargo on American goods, Mr Hughes? I do not think they would take us seriously. A lack of Chevrolets being imported to Beirut? No, regrettably there are people who only understand certain kinds of pressure. The world is only advanced ...'

'... by killing people? A cheerful philosophy.'

'The world is not a cheerful place. I would have thought your investigations into the ancient civilizations would have taught you that. But anyway ... I have decided to take your advice. We shall explain to the passengers what is happening. How they are mixed up in history. What that history is.'

'I'm sure they'll appreciate that.' Franklin felt queasy. 'Tell them what's going on.'

'Exactly. You see, at four o'clock it will become necessary to ... to start killing them. Naturally we hope it will not be necessary. But if it is ... You are right, things must be explained to them if it is possible. Even a soldier knows why he is fighting. It is fair that the passengers be told as well.'

'But they're not fighting.' The Arab's tone, as much as what he said, riled Franklin. 'They're civilians. They're on holiday. They're not fighting.'

'There are no civilians any more,' replied the Arab. 'Your governments pretend, but that is not the case. Those nuclear weapons of yours, they are only to be let off against an army? The Zionists, at least, understand this. All their people are fighting. To kill a Zionist civilian is to kill a soldier.'

'Look, there aren't any Zionist civilians on the ship, for Christ's sake. They're people like poor old Mr Talbot who's lost his passport and has been turned into an American.'

'All the more reason why things must be explained.'

'I see,' said Franklin, and he let the sneer come through. 'So you're going to assemble the passengers and explain to them how they're all really Zionist soldiers and that's why you've got to kill them.'

'No, Mr Hughes, you misunderstand. I am not going to explain anything. They would not listen. No, Mr Hughes, *you* are going to explain things to them.'

'Me?' Franklin didn't feel nervous. Indeed, he felt decisive. 'Certainly not. You can do your own dirty work.'

'But Mr Hughes, you are a public speaker. I have heard you, if only for a short time. You do it so well. You could introduce a historical view of the matter. My second-in-command will give you all the information you require.'

'I don't require any information. Do your own dirty work.'

'Mr Hughes, I really cannot negotiate in two directions at the same time. It is nine-thirty. You have half an hour to decide. At ten you will say that you do the lecture. You will then have two hours, three hours if that is required, with my second-in-command for the briefing.' Franklin was shaking his head, but the Arab continued regardless. 'Then you have until three

investigation systematic search

queasy sick, uneasy

to rile (ifml) to stir up anger

Zionist religious and political organisation behind the establishment of Israel

sneer facial expression showing contempt

decisive resolute

regardless in spite of everything

o'clock to prepare the lecture. I suggest that you make it last forty-five minutes. I shall listen to you, of course, with the greatest interest and attention. And at three-forty-five, if I am satisfied with how you explain matters, we shall in return accept the Irish nationality of your recently married wife. That is all I have to say, you will send me your reply at ten o'clock.'

Back in the stateroom with the Swedes and the Japanese, Franklin remembered a TV series about psychology he'd once been asked to present. It had folded directly after the pilot, a loss nobody much regretted. One item in that show reported an experiment for measuring the point at which self-interest takes over from altruism. Put like this, it sounded almost respectable; but Franklin had been revolted by the actual test. The researchers had taken a female monkey who had recently given birth and put her in a special cage. The mother was still feeding and grooming her infant in a way presumably not too dissimilar from the maternal behaviour of the experimenters' wives. Then they turned a switch and began heating up the metal floor of the monkey's cage. At first she jumped around in discomfort, then squealed a lot, then took to standing on alternate legs, all the while holding her infant in her arms. The floor was made hotter, the monkey's pain more evident. At a certain point the heat from the floor became unbearable, and she was faced with a choice, as the experimenters put it, between altruism and self-interest. She either had to suffer extreme pain and perhaps death in order to protect her offspring, or else place her infant on the floor and stand on it to keep herself from harm.

In every case, sooner or later self-interest had triumphed over altruism.

Franklin had been sickened by the experiment, and glad the TV series hadn't got beyond the pilot, if that was what he would have had to present. Now he felt a bit like that monkey. He was being asked to choose between two equally repellent ideas: that of abandoning his girlfriend while retaining his integrity, or rescuing his girlfriend by justifying to a group of innocent people why it was right that they should be killed. And would that rescue Trish? Franklin hadn't even been promised his own safety; perhaps the pair of them, reclassified as Irish, would merely be moved to the bottom of the killing list, but still remain on it. Who would they start with? The Americans, the British? If they started with the Americans, how long would that delay the killing of the British? Fourteen, sixteen Americans – he translated that brutally into seven or

pilot first programme to test viewer reaction
item segment

altruism attitude opposite to egotism

The function of the monkey episode – a study in human behaviour?

repellent causing disgust, objectionable

Trish see Tricia

eight hours. If they started at four, and the governments stood firm, by midnight they would start killing the British. What order would they do it in? Men first? Random? Alphabetical? Trish's surname was Maitland. Right in the middle of the alphabet. Would she see the dawn?

He imagined himself standing on Tricia's body to protect his own burning feet and shuddered. He would have to do the lecture. That was the difference between a monkey and a human being. In the last analysis, humans were capable of altruism. This was why he was not a monkey. Of course, it was more than probable that when he gave the lecture his audience would conclude the exact opposite – that Franklin was operating out of self-interest, saving his own skin by a foul piece of subservience. But this was the thing about altruism, it was always liable to be misunderstood. And he could explain everything to them all afterwards. If there was an afterwards. If there was a them all.

When the second-in-command arrived, Franklin asked to see the leader again. He intended demanding safe-conduct for Tricia and himself in exchange for the lecture. However, the second-in-command had only come for a reply, not for renewed conversation. Dully, Franklin nodded his head. He'd never been much good at negotiating anyway.

At two-forty-five Franklin was taken to his cabin and allowed to wash. At three o'clock he entered the lecture hall to find the most attentive audience he had ever faced. He filled a glass from the carafe of stale water that nobody had bothered to change. He sensed below him the swell of exhaustion, a rip-tide of panic. After only a day the men seemed almost bearded, the women crumpled. They had already begun not to look like themselves, or the selves that Franklin had spent ten days with. Perhaps this made them easier to kill.

Before he got his own writing credit Franklin had become expert at presenting the ideas of others as plausibly as possible. But never had he felt such apprehension at a script; never had a director imposed such conditions; never had his fee been so bizarre. When first agreeing to the task he had persuaded himself that he could surely find a way of tipping off his audience that he was acting under duress. He would think up some ploy like that of the false Minoan inscriptions; or he would make his lecture so exaggerated, pretend such enthusiasm for the cause thrust upon him, that nobody could possibly miss the irony. No, that wouldn't work. 'Irony,' an ancient TV producer had once confided to him, 'may be defined as what people miss.' And the passengers certainly wouldn't be on the

foul revolting, offensive
subservience *Unterwürfigkeit*
liable to here: likely

attentive paying attention
stale not fresh
exhaustion at the end of one's powers
to exhaust, exhausting
rip-tide dangerous (meeting of currents)
crumpled crushed together
writing credit appointment as a TV author
apprehension fearful expectation

duress unavoidable force or threat
ploy clever trick

ancient very old, senior to

briefing short information session

deviation change of original way or plan, etc.

Before you read: If you were in Franklin's position, how would you address your audience and explain the situation?

residual small amount left over after the rest is taken away

bowler player who throws the ball in cricket

Balfour Declaration made by the British Foreign Secretary Arthur James Balfour in 1917 supporting the Jews in their policy to set up a state in Palestine.

lookout for it in their present circumstances. The briefing had made things yet harder: the second-in-command had given precise instructions, and added that any deviation from them would result not just in Miss Maitland remaining British, but in Franklin's Irish passport no longer being recognized. They certainly knew how to negotiate, these bastards.

'I had been hoping,' he began, 'that the next time I addressed you I would be taking up again the story of Knossos. Unfortunately, as you are aware, the circumstances have changed. We have visitors amongst us.' He paused and looked down the aisle at the leader, who stood before the double doors with a guard on each side. 'Things are different. We are in the hands of others. Our ... destiny is no longer our own.' Franklin coughed. This wasn't very good. Already he was straying into euphemism. The one duty, the one intellectual duty he had, was to speak as directly as he could. Franklin would freely admit he was a showman and would stand on his head in a bucket of herrings if that would raise viewing figures a few thousand; but there was a residual feeling in him – a mixture of admiration and shame – which made him hold in special regard those communicators who were deeply unlike him: the ones who spoke quietly, in their own simple words, and whose stillness gave them authority. Franklin, who knew he could never be like them, tried to acknowledge their example as he spoke.

'I have been asked to explain things to you. To explain how you – we – find ourselves in the position we are now in. I am not an expert on the politics of the Middle East, but I shall try to make things as clear as I can. We should perhaps begin by going back to the nineteenth century, long before the establishment of the state of Israel ...' Franklin found himself back in an easy rhythm, a bowler pitching on a length. He felt his audience begin to relax. The circumstances were unusual, but they were being told a story, and they were offering themselves to the story-teller in the manner of audiences down the ages, wanting to see how things turned out, wanting to have the world explained to them. Hughes sketched in an idyllic nineteenth century, all nomads and goat-farming and traditional hospitality which allowed you to stay in someone else's tent for three days before being asked what the purpose of your visit might be. He talked of early Zionist settlers and Western concepts of land-ownership. The Balfour Declaration. Jewish immigration from Europe. The Second World War. European guilt over the Holocaust being paid for by the Arabs. The Jews having learned from their persecution by the Nazis that the only way to survive was to be like Nazis. Their militarism, expansionism, racism. Their pre-emptive attack on the Egyptian air force at the start of the Six Day War being the exact moral equivalent of Pearl Harbor (Franklin deliberately did not look at the Japanese – or the Americans – at this moment, nor for some time thereafter). The refugee camps. The theft of land. The artificial support of the Israeli economy by the dollar. The atrocities committed against the dispossessed. The Jewish lobby in America. The Arabs only asking from the Western powers for the same justice in the Middle East as had already been accorded to the Jews. The regrettable necessity of violence, a lesson taught the Arabs by the Jews, just as it had been taught the Jews by the Nazis.

Franklin had used up two thirds of his time. If he could feel a brooding hostility in some parts of the audience, there was also, strangely, a wider drowsiness, as if they'd heard this story before and had not believed it then either. 'And so we come to the here and now.' That brought them back to full attention; despite the circumstances, Franklin felt a bubble of pleasure. He was the hypnotist who snaps his fingers. 'In the Middle East, we must understand, there are no civilians any more. The Zionists understand this, the Western governments do not. We, alas, are not civilians. The Zionists have made this happen. You – we – are being held hostage by the Black Thunder group to secure the release of three of their members. You may remember' (though Franklin doubted it, since incidents of this kind were frequent, almost interchangeable) 'that two years ago a civilian aircraft carrying three members of the Black Thunder group was forced down by the American air force in Sicily, that the Italian authorities in contravention of international law compounded this act of piracy by arresting the three freedom fighters, that Britain defended America's action at the United Nations, and that the three men are now in prison in France and Germany. The Black Thunder group does not turn the other cheek, and this legitimate ... hijack' – Franklin used the word carefully, with a glance at the leader as if to demonstrate how he disdained euphemism – 'is in response to that act of piracy. Unfortunately the Western governments do not show the same concern for their citizens as the Black Thunder group shows for its freedom fighters. Unfortunately they are so far declining to release the prisoners. Regrettably the Black Thunder group has no alternative but to carry out its intended threat which was made very clear from the beginning to the Western governments ...'

At this moment a large, unathletic American in a blue shirt got to his feet and started running down the aisle towards the

pre-emptive attacking before being attacked

dispossessed having lost one's home

to accord sth to to give sth to sb
according to, accordance, accordant

contravention violation
to compound here: to make worse

to disdain to reject with contempt

to decline to refuse politely
to release to set free

Arabs. Their guns had not been set to fire only one shot at a time. The noise was very loud and immediately there was a lot of blood. An Italian sitting in the line of fire received a bullet in the head and fell across his wife's lap. A few people got up and quickly sat down again. The leader of the Black Thunder group looked at his watch and waved at Hughes to continue. Franklin took a long swig of stale water. He wished it were something stronger. 'Because of the stubbornness of the Western governments,' he went on, trying to sound now more like an official spokesman than Franklin Hughes, 'and their reckless disregard for human life, it is necessary for sacrifices to be made. You will have understood the historical inevitability of this from what I have said before. The Black Thunder group has every confidence that the Western governments will swiftly come to the negotiating table. In a final effort to make them do so it will be necessary to execute two of you ... of us ... every hour until that point. The Black Thunder group finds this course of action regrettable, but the Western governments leave them no alternative. The order of executions has been decided according to the guilt of the Western nations for the Situation in the Middle East.' Franklin could no longer look at his audience. He dropped his voice, yet could not avoid being heard as he went on. 'Zionist Americans first. Then other Americans. Then British. Then French, Italians and Canadians.'

'What the fuck has Canada ever done in the Middle East? What the fuck?' shouted a man still wearing a towelling maple-leaf hat. He was restrained from getting up by his wife. Franklin, who felt the heat from the metal floor of his cage to be unendurable, shuffled his notes together automatically, stepped off the podium without looking at anyone, walked up the aisle, getting blood on his crêpe soles as he stepped past the dead American, ignored the three Arabs, who could shoot him if they wanted to, and went without escort or opposition to his cabin. He locked the door and lay down on his bunk.

Ten minutes later there came the noise of shooting. From five o'clock to eleven o'clock, punctually on the hour like some terrible parody of a municipal clock, gunfire pealed. Splashes followed, as the bodies were flung over the rail in pairs. Shortly after eleven, twenty-two members of the American Special Forces, who had been trailing the *Santa Euphemia* for fifteen hours, managed to get on board. In the battle six more passengers, including Mr Talbot, the honorary American citizen from Kidderminster, were shot dead. Out of the eight visitors who had helped load supplies at Rhodes, five were killed, two after they had surrendered.

swig large swallow or gulp of liquid
stubbornness inflexibility
sacrifice sth that is given up for a higher cause
inevitability sth that has to happen
unendurable impossible to tolerate
to peal to sound loudly
to surrender to give o. s. up

Neither the leader nor the second-in-command survived, so there remained no witness to corroborate Franklin Hughes's story of the bargain he had struck with the Arabs. Tricia Maitland, who had become Irish for a few hours without realizing it, and who in the course of Franklin Hughes's lecture had returned her ring to the finger where it originally belonged, never spoke to him again.

to corroborate to confirm

What is the narrative purpose for why the two Arab leaders do not survive?

How would you interpret Tricia's reaction?

Migration and ethnicity: Two American views

Thomas Sowell, The American Mosaic

After a teaching career at Cornell, Amherst University and UCLA, Thomas Sowell is currently a Senior Fellow at Stanford University as well as a very influential political commentator in the leading national newspapers and magazines. The following excerpt has been taken from the first chapter of *Ethnic America.* His other works are *Race and Culture* and *Migrations and Cultures.*

The peopling of America is one of the great dramas in all of human history. Over the years, a massive stream of humanity – 45 million people – crossed every ocean and continent to reach the United States. They came speaking every language and representing every nationality, race, and religion. Today, there are more people of Irish ancestry in the United States than in Ireland, more Jews than in Israel, more blacks than in most African countries. There are more people of Polish ancestry in Detroit than in most of the leading cities in Poland, and more than twice as many people of Italian ancestry in New York as in Venice.

How does Sowell illustrate migration to and in America as "one of the greatest dramas in all of human history"?

The sheer magnitude of American ethnic communities makes them autonomous cultures with lives of their own – neither copies of some "mainstream" model nor mere overseas branches of some other country's culture. Chow mein, the St. Patrick's Day parade, and the Afro hairdo all originated on *American* soil. Far from taking direction from overseas, American ethnic communities have supplied leadership to their countries of origin. The first president of Ireland, Eamon de Valera, was born in Brooklyn. Israeli Prime Minister Golda

Give examples for the variety of different ethnic groups.

Chow mein Chinese stew consisting of meat and vegetables

Meir was born in Milwaukee. Liberia was for more than a century ruled by the descendants of freed American Negro slaves.

The massive ethnic communities that make up the mosaic of American society cannot be adequately described as "minorities." There is no "majority." The largest single identifiable ethnic strain are people of British ancestry – who make up just 15 percent of the American population. They barely outnumber German Americans (13 percent) or blacks (11 percent). Millions of Americans cannot identify themselves at all ethnically, due to intermixtures over the generations.

The setting in which the history of all these people unfolded is no less impressive than the numbers and varieties of the people themselves. The United States is one of the largest cultural-linguistic units in the history of the world. From San Francisco to Boston is the same distance as from Madrid to Moscow. Yet here there is one language, one set of laws, and one economy in an area that, in Europe, is fragmented into a multitude of nations, languages, and competing military and political blocs. The size and cohesion of the American society are all the more remarkable because of the diverse origins of the people who make it up. As a unified nation, the United States is older than Germany or Italy. As for size, Texas is larger than France, Colorado is larger than Great Britain, and Italy is only two-thirds the size of California. The United States as a whole is larger than the Roman Empire at its greatest expansion.

to fragment to divide up, to separate

cohesion the state of sticking together

The mixture of unity and diversity runs through American history as through American society today. No ethnic group has been wholly unique, and yet no two are completely alike. Each group has its own geographic distribution pattern, reflecting-conditions when they arrived on American soil and the evolution of the industries and regions to which they became attached. Even the ages of American ethnic groups vary widely. Mexican Americans and Puerto Ricans have median ages of less than twenty years, while the average Irish American or Italian American is more than thirty years old, and Jewish Americans are over forty. These age differences reflect not only current fertility patterns – some groups are composed disproportionately of children – but also historic *changes* in fertility patterns that have caused the successive generations to be of drastically altered size in some groups.

fertility capacity to reproduce

pattern model

Incomes, occupations, and unemployment rates differ substantially among American ethnic groups, as do rates of crime, fertility, and business ownership. The *explanation* of those differences is complex and in many ways surprising. None of the easy explanations fits all the facts. Color has obviously played a major role in determining the fate of many Americans, and yet a black ethnic group like the West Indians earns more than a predominantly white ethnic group like the Puerto Ricans, and the Japanese earn more than whites in general. The initial wealth of a group and its time of arrival are obviously important, as many wealthy "old families" show, but the Jews arrived late and penniless in the nineteenth century and are now more affluent than any other ethnic group.

affluent rich

The economic picture

Comment on what the economic picture reveals.

The incomes, occupations, and unemployment rates of American ethnic groups are too different from one another to be described by any generalization. Moreover, it is as misleading in the economic area as in other areas to think of them as "minorities" who fall below some "majority," or national average, in socioeconomic terms. A number of ethnic groups exceed the national average in socioeconomic status.

Family Income Index (US. Average = 100)

Jewish	172	Total U.S.	100
Japanese	132	Filipino	99
Polish	115	West Indian	94
Chinese	112	Mexican	76
Italian	112	Puerto Rican	63
German	107	Black	62
Anglo-Saxon	107	Indian	60
Irish	103		

Source: U.S. Bureau of the Census and National Jewish Population Survey, 1978.

Samuel P. Huntington, A Plea for Assimilation

Few scholarly books have stimulated such a public discussion as Samuel P. Huntington's *The Clash of Civilizations and the Remaking of World Order,* published in 1996. The Harvard Professor in his long career has also held high positions in the Carter administration where he was responsible for security planning. He is also the President of the American Political Science Association.

In the mid-1990s the West had many characteristics Quigley identified as those of a mature civilization on the brink of decay. Economically the West was far richer than any other

Mark the terms used to sketch the general condition of the Western civilization.

civilization, but it also had low economic growth rates, saving rates, and investment rates, particularly as compared with the societies of East Asia. Individual and collective consumption had priority over the creation of the capabilities for future economic and military power. Natural population growth was low, particularly compared with that of Islamic countries. Neither of these problems, however, would inevitably have catastrophic consequences. Western economies were still growing; by and large Western peoples were becoming better off; and the West was still the leader in scientific research and technological innovation. Low birth rates were unlikely to be cured by governments (whose efforts to do so are generally even less successful than their efforts to reduce population growth). Immigration, however, was a potential source of new vigor and human capital provided two conditions were met: first, if priority were given to able, qualified, energetic people with the talents and expertise needed by the host country; second, if the new migrants and their children were assimilated into the cultures of the country and the West. The United States was likely to have problems meeting the first condition and European countries problems meeting the second. Yet setting policies governing the levels, sources, characteristics, and assimilation of immigrants is well within the experience and competence of Western governments.

vigor energy, power
provided on the condition
to assimilate to make similar, alike

Far more significant than economics and demography are problems of moral decline, cultural suicide, and political disunity in the West. Oft-pointed-to manifestations of moral decline include:

decline going down

1. increases in antisocial behavior, such as crime, drug use, and violence generally;
2. family decay, including increased rates of divorce, illegitimacy, teen-age pregnancy, and single-parent families;
3. at least in the United States, a decline in "social capital," that is, membership in voluntary associations and the interpersonal trust associated with such membership;
4. general weakening of the "work ethic" and rise of a cult of personal indulgence;
5. decreasing commitment to learning and intellectual activity, manifested in the United States in lower levels of scholastic achievement.

illegitimacy children born to unmarried parents
indulgence *Nachsicht, Nachgiebigkeit*
assertion claims

The future health of the West and its influence on other societies depends in considerable measure on its success in coping with those trends, which, of course, give rise to the assertions of moral superiority by Muslims and Asians.

Comment on the examples given for the multicultural threat that is endangering the United States.

Western culture is challenged by groups within Western societies. One such challenge comes from immigrants from other civilizations who reject assimilation and continue to adhere to and to propagate the values, customs, and cultures of their home societies. This phenomenon is most notable among Muslims in Europe, who are, however, a small minority. It is also manifest, in lesser degree, among Hispanics in the United States, who are a large minority. If assimilation fails in this case, the United States will become a cleft country, with all the potentials for internal strife and disunion that entails. In Europe, Western civilization could also be undermined by the weakening of its central component, Christianity. Declining proportions of Europeans profess religious beliefs, observe religious practices, and participate in religious activities. This trend reflects not so much hostility to religion as indifference to it. Christian concepts, values, and practices nonetheless pervade European civilization. "Swedes are probably the most unreligious people in Europe," one of them commented, "but you cannot understand this country at all unless you realize that our institutions, social practices, families, politics, and way of life are fundamentally shaped by our Lutheran heritage." Americans, in contrast to Europeans, overwhelmingly believe in God, think themselves to be religious people, and attend church in large numbers. While evidence of a resurgence of religion in America was lacking as of the mid-1980s the following decade seemed to witness intensified religious activity. The erosion of Christianity among Westerners is likely to be at worst only a very long term threat to the health of Western civilization.

A more immediate and dangerous challenge exists in the United States. Historically American national identity has been defined culturally by the heritage of Western civilization and politically by the principles of the American Creed on which Americans overwhelmingly agree: liberty, democracy, individualism, equality before the law, constitutionalism, private property. In the late twentieth century both components of American identity have come under concentrated and sustained onslaught from a small but influential number of intellectuals and publicists. In the name of multiculturalism they have attacked the identification of the United States with Western civilization, denied the existence of a common American culture, and promoted racial, ethnic, and other subnational cultural identities and groupings. They have denounced, in the words of one of their reports, the "systematic bias toward European culture and its derivatives" in education and "the dom-

to propagate to spread, pass on

manifest clear

to entail to have as a consequence

to profess to openly declare faith in

to pervade to be present throughout

resurgence revival

What according to Huntington is to be done to meet the challenges?

sustained prolonged

onslaught attack

to denounce to proclaim as evil

bias preference

derivative sth based on sth else

ethnocentric focused on one's ethnicity
separatist sb insisting on separation
to divest to strip or dispossess

inheritance what one gets from one's ancestors
to inherit, heritage; heir

redemptive saving from sin
to redeem, redeemer, redemption

e pluribus unum (Lat.) "Out of many, one."

tangle a twisted mass
to squabble to quarrel noisily

assiduous careful, diligent

to disavow to deny

inance of the European-American monocultural perspective." The multiculturalists are, as Arthur M. Schlesinger, Jr., said, "very often ethnocentric separatists who see little in the Western heritage other than Western crimes." Their "mood is one of divesting Americans of the sinful European inheritance and seeking redemptive infusions from non-Western cultures."

The multicultural trend was also manifested in a variety of legislation that followed the civil rights acts of the 1960s, and in the 1990s the Clinton administration made the encouragement of diversity one of its major goals. The contrast with the past is striking. The Founding Fathers saw diversity as a reality and as a problem: hence the national motto, *e pluribus unum*, chosen by a committee of the Continental Congress consisting of Benjamin Franklin, Thomas Jefferson, and John Adams. Later political leaders who also were fearful of the dangers of racial, sectional, ethnic, economic, and cultural diversity (which, indeed, produced the largest war of the century between 1815 and 1914), responded to the call of "bring us together," and made the promotion of national unity their central responsibility. "The one absolutely certain way of bringing this nation to ruin, of preventing all possibility of its continuing as a nation at all," warned Theodore Roosevelt, "would be to permit it to become a tangle of squabbling nationalities." In the 1990s, however, the leaders of the United States have not only permitted that but assiduously promoted the diversity rather than the unity of the people they govern.

The leaders of other countries have, as we have seen, at times attempted to disavow their cultural heritage and shift the identity of their country from one civilization to another. In no case to date have they succeeded and they have instead created schizophrenic torn countries. The American multiculturalists similarly reject their country's cultural heritage. Instead of attempting to identify the United States with another civilization, however, they wish to create a country of many civilizations, which is to say a country not belonging to any civilization and lacking a cultural core. History shows that no country so constituted can long endure as a coherent society. A multicivilizational United States will not be the United States; it will be the United Nations.

Self-assessment

Fill in the dialogue to complete the cartoon.

Biographies

John Agard (*1949) was born in British Guiana, now Guayana. He moved to England in 1977 and became a touring lecturer visiting schools in the UK to promote a better understanding of Caribbean culture. He has published several volumes of poetry and also children's books and anthologies of poems from all over the world.

Gloria Anzaldúa (1942–2004) born in Texas, was a feminist poet and fiction writer. She was editor of various anthologies of programmatic works such as *This Bridge Called My Back: Writings by Radical Women of Color* (1981) and *this bridge we call home: radical visions for transformation* (2002). She also wrote bilingual children's books and taught Chicano Studies and Feminist Studies at University of Texas, San Francisco State University and the University of California at Santa Cruz.

Julian Barnes (*1946) was born in Leicester and educated at the City of London School and Magdalen College, Oxford. After working as a lexicographer on the Oxford English Dictionary, he took up journalism writing for the New Statesman and the Sunday Times before becoming the television critic for The Observer. His novels, among others *Flaubert's Parrot* (1984) and *A History of the World in 10½ Chapters* (1989) have won international acclaim.

Michael Blake (*1945), a native of Fort Bragg, NC, lived for a while in Texas before finally settling in California where he now lives with his wife and three small children. He started writing for periodicals before he turned to fiction and, encouraged by the actor Kevin Costner, wrote a novel about the Indians, *Dances with Wolves* (1988), which he later turned into a screenplay for the blockbuster film *Dances with Wolves.* A sequel to that novel, *The Holy Road,* appeared in 2001.

T. Coraghessan Boyle (*1948), born in Peekskill, NY, went to the University of Iowa to study Nineteenth Century British Literature and later English and History before taking up teaching English at the University of Southern California. All of the sixteen novels he has written take a critical look at present-day-America, especially at the role of ethnic minorities as in *The Tortilla Curtain* (1995) or *East Is East* (1990).

Lan Cao (*1963), born in Vietnam, left her native country in 1975 and now lives in New York, where she is a professor of International Law at Brooklyn Law School. Her novel *Monkey Bridge* (1997), dedicated to her mother, is an autobiographic narrative of her life in Vietnam, the Vietnam War, their escape and the challenges of settling down in a new world in the United States. In the novel, she continuously compares her own way of coping with the new reality with her mother's coping strategies.

Sandra Cisneros (*1954) was born in Chicago and works as a novelist, poet and essayist. She went to Loyola University in Chicago and to the University of Iowa. In her work she writes about her experience as a Latina woman in a male Anglo world. Poverty, illiteracy, alienation, ethnic friction and discrimination against women have been her central topics. In addition to her writing, she has lectured at many prestigious American universities and is an active Pen member. Her work has been highly praised by literary critics and widely accepted by the public.

Waring Cuney (1906–1976), born in Washington, D.C., to a middle-class African-American family, went to Armstrong High School and Howard University, where he took up music. He made friends with Langston Hughes and became a member of the Harlem Renaissance. Little is known about his work, but the poem "Images", also set to music, has made him immortal.

Abelardo Delgado (1930–2004), born in Chihuahua, Mexico, grew up in the border town of El Paso where he went to university and graduated in Spanish Studies. He also got married there and he and his wife had eight children. Apart from writing poetry, he committed himself to teaching Chicano Studies and setting up Spanish speaking radio stations. For these reasons, he became a source of inspiration to many Chicano leaders and writers.

David Guterson (*1956) was born in Seattle, where he completed a B.A. in English Literature and an M.A. in Creative Writing at the University of Washington. He then taught English at the local high school in Bainbridge Island in Puget Sound – an area whose nature and history have greatly influenced his writing. Later, he started as a Sports journalist and contributor to Harper's magazine before writing novels. His greatest success so far has been *Snow Falling on Cedars* which was also turned into a successful film.

Langston Hughes (1902–1967) was born in Joplin, Missouri. In the early 1920s, he entered Columbia University, but left it soon after to travel to Europe. Upon his return, he held various jobs and went to Lincoln University in Pennsylvania where he graduated with a B.A. degree. He published poetry and was one of the leaders of the Harlem Renaissance and an established artist with worldwide fame. Over time, his writing became more political, even radical, and increasingly conscious of its African roots. In 1937, during the Spanish Civil War, he served as a newspaper correspondent and became a friend of Ernest Hemingway.

Samuel P. Huntington (*1927) is a professor at Harvard University and a leading American political scientist, who has been an influential adviser to different American administrations. His central thesis is that in the 21st century the most significant political forces will be civilisations rather than national states. His views have strongly influenced the political debate on immigration worldwide.

Harriet Ann Jacobs (1813–1897) was among the few African-American women to work as a writer and political activist in the 19th century. Her autobiographical narrative on her life as a slave girl is both an authentic report on the conditions of slavery and a passionate fight for emancipation. She further rebelled against the traditional value system by choosing a white man as the protector of her family and her children.

Hanif Kureishi (*1954) was born in Bromley as the son of a Pakistani immigrant and an English woman. Within his family and the neighbourhood, he experienced the ethnic and cultural clashes which are characteristic of his novels and his plays. *My Beautiful Laundrette* (1985) about a gay Pakistani immigrant and his white lover was his first success, even though it received criticism from the Pakistani side which felt misinterpreted. He took up the same theme and constellation of characters in *The Buddha of Suburbia* and *The Black Album.*

Harper Lee (*1926) was born in Monroeville, southwest Alabama. She first studied at Huntingdon College, then took law at the University of Alabama and even attended Oxford University for a year. In 1960, she published *To Kill a Mockingbird,* her only book. This courtroom novel actually treats two topics, that of growing up and that of a trial against an African-American man falsely accused of raping a white girl. The film version of the novel with Gregory Peck as the father Atticus Finch added to the author's fame.

Bernard Malamud (1914–1986) was born in Brooklyn and was one of the most prominent Jewish-American novelists of the last century. He was educated at the City College of New York and at Columbia University and then took up teaching at Bennington College. That he was a master of subtle, humorous storytelling is best reflected in his collections of short stories, *The Magic Barrel* (1958) and *Idiots First* (1963). His novels dealing with being a Jew in America include *The Assistant* (1957) and *The Fixer* (1966).

Anchee Min (*1957) was born in Shanghai. After a career in communal farming and later the Chinese propaganda film industry, she fell into disgrace and left China for the United States in 1983. Her autobiographical novel *Red Azalea* (1993) was well received and followed by *Katherine* (1995). Anchee Min is also a successful painter, photographer and musician and lives in both Chicago and Shanghai.

Simon J. Ortiz (*1941) is a native American writer of poems, short stories, essays and children's books. He grew up in Acoma Pueblo in Albuquerque, New Mexico, and was strongly influenced by the oral tradition of his native American family and community. Already from an early age, he experienced how difficult, sometimes impossible, it was to unite his native culture with the English culture imposed on him and those around him both in school and in public life.

Arundhati Roy (*1961) was born in Bengal, India, and grew up in Kerala, a province with a considerable number of Christians although they are in the minority. She thus came into contact with the Western world represented by the state and church authorities. After her university degree at the Delhi School of Architecture, she turned to screenwriting instead and worked for the Indian film industry. She is married to an Indian film-maker. Her only novel so far, *The God of Small Things* (1997), won the Booker Prize and became an international bestseller.

Buffy Sainte-Marie (*1941) is a Canadian First Nations musician, composer, educator and activist. Born on a Cree reservation in the Qu'Appelle Valley, Saskatchewan, she was later adopted and moved to the States, where she grew up in Maine and Massachusetts. There she went to university and got her Ph.D. in Fine Arts. She also holds a degree in Oriental Philosophy. A prominent writer and performer of protest songs, she has written numerous songs which have been performed by artists such as among others Cher, Joe Cocker, Neil Diamond, Janis Joplin, Elvis Presley and Barbra Streisand.

Thomas Sowell (*1930) holds university degrees from Harvard, Columbia and a Ph.D. from the University of Chicago. He previously taught as Professor of Economics at UCLA and Amherst College and now works as a Senior Fellow at Stanford University. He has written numerous books on migration, race relationships and ethnic America and is a very influential political commentator.

Atima Srivastava (*1961) was born in Mumbai (Bombay), India, and moved to England when she was eight. She now lives in London. Her two novels, *Transmission* and *Looking for Maya,* reflect her biography and are characterised by intercultural friction and a young "hybrid" woman's search for her identity. They have not only been very successful, they have even made it into the syllabus of some British and other European universities and school examining boards.

Meera Syal (*1963) was born in England and went to Manchester University to study English and Drama. While still at university she was the co-author of a popular TV-series. She is a woman of many talents, a novelist, a writer of screenplays, an actress and a journalist regularly contributing to The Guardian. All of her work, like her highly praised first novel *Anita and Me* (1996), is based on her experience as a girl or a woman between two worlds trying to mediate between them.

Gay Talese (*1932) is a second-generation Italian, born in Ocean City, New Jersey, where he grew up as an Italian-Catholic boy in an Irish-Catholic parish on a Protestant island. This minority-feeling has become a trademark of his writing in which he combines literary themes and techniques with the matter-of-fact presentation of journalism. The main characters of his stories and reports are representatives of the hidden and often neglected majority whom he observes in detail and with fondness and sympathy.

Amy Tan (*1952) was born in Oakland, California, as the daughter of Chinese immigrants who had left China in the time of the Civil War. She got her M.A. in English and Linguistics from San José State University. Later she specialised in training developmentally-disabled children before setting up a firm writing speeches for executives. Before preparing for a new career as a novelist, she took her mother to China, which was both an eye-opener for her and a source of inspiration for her novel *The Joy Luck Club* (1989).

Kurt Vonnegut, Jr. (*1922) was born in Indianapolis to German-American parents. He went to Cornell University to major in Chemistry, then joined the U.S. Army and served in Germany where he became a prisoner of war and witnessed the bombing of Dresden. Vonnegut is still well known for his satirical and pessimistic writing and for his combination of utopian elements in literature and science fiction and a general criticism of Western civilisation, cf. *Slaughterhouse Five* (1969) and *Cat's Cradle* (1963).

Developing skills

Useful words and phrases

- **action** what happens in a story or a play
  - a course of action
  - to perform an action
  - to carry out an action

- **allusion** indirect, brief or unclear reference
  - sth is an allusion to
  - to make an allusion to
  - the text contains allusions to
  - this is an obvious/obscure allusion to

- **to appeal** to attract sb's interest
  - the author does not succeed in appealing to his readers

- **appreciation** a judgement that is typically positive
  - to show an appreciation of
  - in appreciation of

- **approach** coming nearer; systematic way
  - an approach to a text

- **argument** (way of presenting) one's idea
  - to use/put forward/advance an argument for or against sth
  - to support an argument
  - to base an argument on sth
  - an argument is (un)convincing/(in)conclusive
  - a strong/weak argument
  - to disprove/refute an argument

- **argumentative** containing arguments, logical
  - an argumentative text, essay, etc.

- **aspect** part, special view
  - the central aspect
  - to refer to a particular aspect
  - to cover certain aspects
  - several aspects are presented

- **atmosphere** arrangement of significant details, e. g. of time and place, meant to arouse a certain mood in the reader or spectator
  – to give sth a peculiar atmosphere
  – to create an atmosphere of
  – to establish/evoke an atmosphere of

- **attitude** way of thinking or feeling, opinion, judgement
  – to point out the author's attitude towards his readers
  – to describe the different attitudes towards sth
  – to have/take/assume/adopt an attitude towards sth
  – to state an attitude
  – to defend an attitude
  – to change one's attitude

- **character** here: literary figure
  – flat ch. = one-sided, easily recognisable literary figure or type showing little or no development
  – round ch. = complex, life-like literary figure
  – a character plays a certain role
  – a character shows/undergoes a certain development

- **to characterise** to endow a figure with certain features, to describe and evaluate certain characteristics

- **characterisation** the drawing of a character in a play or novel
  – to give/write a characterisation of

- **chronological order** arrangement following the natural order of time

- **climax** highest point of interest, crisis in the development of events, point of culmination
  – sth is the climax of
  – sth leads up to/rises to/reaches a climax
  – to use sth as a climax
  – this event is the climax of the story

- **to comment on** to give opinions on sth

- **conclusion** belief or opinion arrived at by reasoning
  – to draw a conclusion from
  – to outline the conclusion drawn by the author
  – to arrive at a conclusion

– to come to the conclusion that
– to jump to conclusions

- **context** passages surrounding an extract, general setting of experience or history
  – to place sth in a wider context

- **contrast** arrangement in opposites
  – the story is structured by contrasts
  – to present a contrast
  – sth forms a contrast to
  – to arrange sth for contrast
  – by contrast with

- **criticism** judgement or opinion on literature, art, etc., typically negative
  – to voice criticism of sth

- **dénouement** in a literary work, esp. a drama, final stage of plot where everything is made clear, solution

- **to describe** to give a detailed account of sth, to give a picture of sth in words
  – to describe sb's character
  – the events described in the story
  – life in town as described above
  – to describe sth/sb as

- **description** the act or result of describing

- **detail** small, significant part
  – descriptive details
  – to point sth out in detail
  – to pay attention to detail

- **development** growth, evolution, gradual change
  – to undergo a development
  – the most important stages in the development
  – to trace sb's development

- **dialect** regional, social or ethnic variant of a language

- **drama** literary work presenting a "story" through dialogue and action, for stage, radio or television performance

- **dramatic sketch** very short form of a one-act-play

- **effect** impression produced on the mind of the reader, spectator, etc.; result, outcome
  – to have/produce an effect on
  – to describe the effect of sth
  – to achieve an effect

- **element** a constituent part of a text

- **emotion** strong feeling, excited state of mind, passion
  – to stir up emotions
  – to be overcome by emotion/by an emotion of joy
  – to experience an outburst of emotion

- **essay** short prose composition, typically casual as to topic and structure
  – argumentative e. = essay mainly based on arguments and their development
  – descriptive e. = essay mainly containing description

- **evaluation** appraisal, judgement

- **example** fact which illustrates a rule or confirms a statement
  – to give an example of
  – to give/quote examples from the text
  – to refer to an example
  – an example demonstrates/illustrates sth

- **exposition** in a drama or a narrative text, the presentation of basic information and constellation of characters

- **figurative language** speaking in images as opposed to direct reference

- **form** the formal presentation of content
  – to describe the outward form of a text
  – to identify the form of a text
  – to impose a form on a text
  – in the form of sth

- **genre** category of literary form, e. g. short story, novel, play, etc.

- **heading** title words at the top of a page or at the beginning of a chapter
  – under the heading of

- **hero/heroine** main character of a narrative or dramatic text

- **image** figure of speech which conveys a picture to the mind
  – the dominating image is/varies throughout the text
  – to speak in images
  – to use/employ/make use of images
  – vivid/ready-made images

- **imagery** extended use of images

- **implication** meaning or consequence which is not directly stated but only hinted at or suggested

- **impression** feeling or image kept in memory
  – to make an impression on
  – to create the impression of authenticity

- **information** (only singular)
  – the text provides information on
  – information is given about

- **informative** supplying information
  – the text is informative

- **intention** aim, purpose, design
  – to describe the author's intention

- **interaction** acting upon each other, interdependence of action
  – linguistic/verbal interaction

- **interpretation** evaluation based on analysis
  – to provide evidence to support an interpretation
  – the terminology of interpretation
  – an interpretation is allegorical/psychological
  – an interpretation is determined by sth
  – to give/make/write an interpretation of
  – an interpretation explains/elucidates the meaning of a text

- **introduction** opening passage or paragraph
  – an introduction to sth

- **irony** way of speaking or writing in which words mean the opposite of their normal or apparent meaning

- **key-word** significant word providing a clue to the meaning of the text

- **language** style of speech or writing
  – different varieties of language
  – special features of the language of a text
  – matter-of-fact/neutral/unemotional/allusive language
  – the regional and social differentiation of language use

- **line** unit of text in a poem or song
  – end-stopped line
  – run-on line

- **metaphor** figure of speech implying but not openly stating a comparison (he was the lion in a battle);
  note that there is *no particle* such as *like* or *as* to express the comparison

- **metre** the basic underlying rhythm of a poem or song

- **to mirror** to reflect/show/reveal
  – the singer's opposition as reflected in the song

- **motif** a theme elaborated in a piece of literature or music

- **motive** the driving force behind actions
  – to have a motive for
  – to be driven by a motive of
  – to act from motives of
  – to explain/trace the motives for sb's behaviour
  – to analyse sb's motives

- **narrator** fictitious character who tells a story

- **non-standard** differing from a standard, use of language not accepted as standard

- **paragraph** division of several lines of writing, starting on a new line

- **passage** short extract from a piece of writing
- **personification** attribution of human characteristics to inanimate objects or abstract ideas
  – to personify the desire for power
- **plot** the organisation of the overall action in a play, a novel or a short story which relates individual actions and motives and consequences
- **poem** piece of writing in verse form
- **point of view** angle from which the author decides to present the story, thus conditioning its reception; ranges from subjective insights to general overview
  – the speaker/narrator has a particular point of view
  – the author presents sth from a specific point of view
- **quotation** exact repetition of another person's words
  – to quote from
- **register** appropriate use of language (choice of words and grammatical structure) according to subject
  – matter, situation, communicative partner
- **rhyme pattern** regularity in identity of sounds or final syllables at the end of lines
- **setting** the physical or spiritual background e. g. of time, place, atmosphere in a literary work
- **simile** figure of speech openly stating a comparison by means of particles such as *like* or *as*
- **slang** words and expressions that belong to informal usage
- **solution** answer to a problem, puzzle, etc.
  – the solution to a problem
  – to seek/find/arrive at a solution
- **stanza** group of lines, usually with a rhyme, forming a unit of a poem
- **to state** to declare/affirm/express in words
  – the reason for violence as stated by the author

- **statement** expression in words
  – to make a statement about sth

- **stereotype** unchanging, formalised image, belief, phrase, idea, etc.

- **structure** the overall design of a text; the way in which the units of meaning are arranged and the elements of plot, action, character, language, etc. are woven together to bring out the theme
  – the text has/shows a particular/simple/complex structure
  – the text is structured by repetition/by contrasts
  – the text is structured thematically

- **style** particular use of language (lexis and grammar) in an author's work, in an epoch
  – to analyse the style of a story

- **stylistic** belonging to style
  – the author uses particular stylistic means/devices

- **to subdivide** to divide a part into smaller parts

- **subject matter** that which is discussed or presented; topic or theme

- **suspense** state of anxious uncertainty and expectation created in and by a literary work
  – to keep the reader in suspense

- **symbol** something concrete existing in its own right which is used to express a more general concept or abstract idea
  – a symbol presents/represents sth
  – a symbol stands for sth
  – the cross is a symbol of
  – sth is presented symbolically
  – the symbolic meaning of
  – the language of symbolism

- **technique** a special way of doing things, of writing
  – to apply a technique
  – a special technique is used/applied by the author

- **tension** excitement, anxiety, suspense
  – to create tension

- tension is built up
- tension rises to a climax
- tension is (abruptly/gradually) released
- tension increases

- **theme** central idea/concept in a literary work
  - to state the theme of a story
  - to represent the theme of a text

- **tone** describes the writer's attitude towards the subject and towards the audience/reader; the tone of a narrative is similar to the tone of a voice, it may be neutral, enthusiastic, mocking , ironical, grave, angry or complacent

- **verse** a poem; one or several lines of a poem/ **free verse** (with lines of varying length, without rhyme)
  - sth is written in verse
  - to write/compose verses
  - to say sth in verse

Acknowledgements

Texts

Bernard Malamud, "The Lady of the Lake" from *The Magic Barrel,* © 1950, 1958, renewed 1977, 1986 by Bernard Malamud. Reprinted by permission of Farrar, Straus and Giroux, LLC, New York 2003, pp. 112–133

Michael Blake, *Dances with Wolves,* copyright © 1988 by Michael Blake, London, Penguin 1988, pp. 203–209

Buffy Sainte-Marie, "Now that the buffalo's gone" from *It's My Way,* Vanguard 1964, © TM-Music Inc./Alley Music Corp./Carlin Music Corp., Greenhorn Musikverlag GmbH, Hamburg

Simon J. Ortiz, "The Killing of a State Cop" from *The Man to Send Rain Clouds,* New York, Penguin 1992 (Vintage Books 1975), pp. 101–108

Gay Talese, "The Bridge" from *New York Observed,* ed. by Barbara Cohen, Seymour Chwast and Steven Heller. New York, Harry N. Abrams Publishers 1987, p. 46

Harriet Jacobs, "Scenes at the Plantation" from *Incidents in the Life of a Slave Girl,* New York and Oxford, Oxford University Press 1988, pp. 131–137

Harper Lee, *To Kill a Mockingbird,* London, Pan Books 1960, pp. 80–82

Waring Cuney, "No Images", from Opportunity Magazine 1, New York 1926

Langston Hughes, "I, too, sing America" from *Selected Poems of Langston Hughes,* New York, Alfred A. Knopf 1965, p. 275

Kurt Vonnegut, Jr., "Adam" from *Welcome to the Monkey House,* London, Jonathan Cape 1969, pp. 276–283

Lan Cao, *The Monkey Bridge,* copyright © 1997 by Lan Cao, used py permission of Viking Penguin, a division of Penguin Group (USA) Inc., London, Penguin 1997, pp. 37–41

Amy Tan, "Rice Husband", from *The Joy Luck Club,* © 1989 by Amy Tan, used by permission of G. P. Putnam's Sons, a division of Penguin Group (USA) Inc., New York, Ivy Books 1989, pp. 168–174

David Guterson, *Snow Falling on Cedars,* copyright © 1994 by David Guterson, reprinted by permission of Harcourt, Inc., New York, Vintage Books 1995, pp. 199–202

Sandra Cisneros, "No Speak English", from *The House on Mango Street,* New York, Vintage Contemporaries 1991 (1984), pp. 76–78

T. Coraghessan Boyle, *The Tortilla Curtain,* London, Bloomsbury 1996, pp. 199–200

Abelardo Delgado, "stupid america" from *Chicano: 25 Pieces of a Chicano Mind,* Austin, Texas University Press 1969, p. 26

Gloria Anzaldúa, "To live in the Borderlands means you" from *Borderlands. La Frontera. The New Mestiza,* San Francisco, Aunt Lute Books 1999, pp. 216–217

Hanif Kureishi, *The Buddha of Suburbia,* London, Faber & Faber 1990, pp. 23–28

Meera Syal, *Anita and Me,* New York, The New Press 1996, pp. 34–36

Atima Srivastava, *Looking for Maya,* London, Quartet Books 1999, pp. 8–11

John Agard, "Checking out me history" from *Life doesn't frighten me at all: Poems,* London, Heinemann 1989, pp. 13–15; "Oxford Don" from *Mangoes and Bullets: Selected and New Poems 1972–84.* London, Pluto Press 1989, p. 44

Anchee Min, *Katherine,* London, Penguin 1996, pp. 77–84

Norman Williams, "Protest", from *Multicultural Scenes for Young Actors* ed. by Craig Slaight and Jack Sharrar, Lyme, NH Smith and Kraus Books 1995, pp. 74–79

Arundhati Roy, "Re-dreaming the dream", from *The God of Small Things,* London, Flamingo 1997, pp. 47–53

Julian Barnes, "The Visitors" from *A History of the World in 10 1/2 Chapters,* copyright © 1989 by Julian Barnes, used py permission of Alfred A. Knopf, a division of Random House, Inc., New York, Alfred A. Knopf 1989, pp. 33–58

Thomas Sowell, "The American Mosaic" from *Ethnic America. A History,* New York, Basic Books 1981, pp. 3–5

Samuel P. Huntington, "A Plea for Assimilation" from *The Clash of Civilizations and the Remaking of World Order,* New York, Simon & Schuster 1996, pp. 304–306

Pictures © 1998 AsianWeek: p. 134 top; © Leonardo Cendamo/Agentur Focus: p. 135 bottom; © dpa: p. 133, p. 137 bottom; dpa-Bildarchiv: p. 138; © dpa-Fotoreport: p. 136 bottom; © dpa-Fotoreport/Andreas Altwein: p. 135 center; © Jiri Rezac/VISUM: p. 137 top; Ralf König: p. 6/7 (cartoon); © Luise Kött-Gärtner, „Sehnsucht": cover; Library of Congress USZ62-43605: p. 135 top; Morris, Lucky Luke reitet für die 20er Kavallerie, Bd. 19, Delta Verlag, Stuttgart 1979, S. 18: p. 132; Reuters: p. 6/7 (photo); United States International Communication Agency: p. 136 top; © Anne Weise: p. 134 center